Transfer Pricing, Multinationals and Taxation

Concepts, Mechanisms and Regulations

About the Book

Global changes in business and tax environments are having profound impact on the volume and value of trade and transfer pricing strategies. A large share of world trade consists of transfer of merchandise and services within multinational enterprises. By following transfer pricing practices carefully, multinational businesses can manage risk while improving operational and financial performance based on a long-term view of sustainable growth.

The development of optimal transfer pricing regulations has become a key accounting issue in the context of Indian economy. The Finance Act, 2001 introduced the detailed Transfer Pricing Regulations (TPR) in India with effect from April I, 2001 corresponding to the assessment year 2002-2003. Absence of such regulations resulted in litigation and loss of revenue to the exchequer.

This book describes and examines various aspects of transfer pricing including import of raw material, other consumable stores, transfer of dividends, royalties, technical fees and other services. It provides an insight into corporate strategies, financial goals and performance evaluation in the context of global and Indian legislations and standards pertaining to transfer pricing. This up-to-date work is useful for post-graduate students, researchers, analysts, tax experts, and corporate executives.

Author's Profile

Dr. Ashok Kumar obtained his M.Com., M.Phil. and Ph.D. degrees from the Department of Commerce, Delhi School of Economics, University of Delhi. He has more than 30 years of teaching experience and 10 years of research experience in the areas of transfer pricing, accounting standards and taxation. He has also presented papers in national seminars of All India Accounting Association. Presently, Dr. Kumar is Reader in the Department of Commerce, PGDAV College (M), University of Delhi, Delhi.

Transfer Pricing, Multinationals and Taxation

Concepts, Mechanisms and Regulations

Ashok Kumar

New Century Publications
New Delhi, India

NEW CENTURY PUBLICATIONS
4800/24, Bharat Ram Road,
Ansari Road, Daryaganj,
New Delhi - 110 002
Tel.: 23247798, 55396605
Telefax: 011-41017798
E-mail: indiatax@vsnl.com
www.newcenturypublications.com

Editorial office:
34, Gujranwala Town, Part-2,
Delhi - 110 009
Tel.: 27247805, 27464774

First Published 2006

ISBN: 81-7708-108-x

Published by New Century Publications and printed at Singhal Print Media, New Delhi -110 005

PRINTED IN INDIA

Preface

Transfer pricing is the practice of establishing arm's length prices for transactions undertaken between organizations belonging to the same multinational corporate group. By considering transfer pricing practices carefully, multinational businesses can manage risk while improving operational and financial performance based on a long-term view of sustainable growth.

International access and globalisation are inextricably linked. Transnational/multinational corporations have been there for about 100 years. With conglomerates within a country and multinationals across the countries being a common phenomenon, sourcing within an organisation is a necessary concomitant.

Despite all the literature which has been built around transfer pricing, no universally applicable method has been devised so far. Just like a therapy is patient-specific so also a transfer pricing strategy is organization-specific. Although arm's length principle has been widely advocated, there are companies all over the world which have adopted different variants thereof and used them to their advantage.

Since the initiation of economic reforms in 1991, the Indian economy has seen the entry of new multinationals (MNCs) into the country. Also, domestic companies are growing into conglomerates by adding new products and locations. A large number of MNCs have made their presence felt on the Indian shores for the first time.

The development of an optimal transfer pricing system has become a key accounting issue. The Finance Act, 2001 introduced the detailed Transfer Pricing Regulations (TPR) in India with effect from April I, 2001 corresponding to the assessment year 2002-2003. The rules for transfer pricing were notified on August 21, 2001. The need for a detailed and separate regulation for administering transfer pricing was felt with the globalisation of the Indian economy. Absence of such regulations resulted in litigation and loss of revenue to the exchequer.

Transfer pricing is an olive green subject. With the growth in the size of companies under the impact of mergers and acquisitions on the one hand and computerised and robotised technology on the other, the subject will witness added interest in the years to come. It will remain an interesting area to explore for many years hence.

The present book is divided into 8 chapters. Chapter 1 is introductory in nature and discusses the practices of intra-corporate transfers. Chapter 2 gives a detailed account of multinationals and conglomerates as a backdrop to understand the nature and behaviour of multinationals. Chapter 3 examines various transfer pricing methods used by such entities depending on their requirements. The case of evaluating the performance of decentralised organisations has been dealt with in Chapter 4. It also discusses the impact of transfer pricing on performance evaluation. International legislations and standards pertaining to transfer pricing are examined in Chapter 5 and that of India in Chapter 6. Taking together, these two chapters constitute the core segment of the book. They provide the legal and accounting framework for transfer pricing at national and international levels. Chapter 7 presents select corporate cases on transfer pricing. This chapter examines the practices being followed in India. The concluding Chapter 8 gives an overall summary besides providing useful suggestions and alternatives.

I wish to express my thanks to Professor B.M. Lall Nigam and Professor R.N. Goyale of the Department of Commerce, Delhi School of Economics, University of Delhi for their continuous support and sustained encouragement. I place on record my deep appreciation for my wife Jai Prabha and sons Nishkarsh and Tarun for bearing with me during the course of the completion of this tedious work.

New Delhi
May 2006

Ashok Kumar

Contents

1

Transfer Pricing – An Overview

A large share of world trade consists of transfer of goods, intangibles and services with Multinational Corporations (MNCs). Determination of right price for these transactions is of great importance of arrive at the correct tax liability in each jurisdiction. Extensive guidelines have been issued by the Organisation for Economic Co-operation and Development (OECD) for determination of the arm's length price in order to avoid economic double taxation and the consequent impediments to world trade. To ensure that the tax base of an MNC is divided fairly, it is important that transfers within a group should approximate those which would be negotiated between independent firms.

It is important to note that transfer pricing is in a sense directly related to the concept of Permanent Establishment (PE). An organisation operating abroad through a PE is taxable on the profits attributable to it. Transfer pricing helps in computing profits of the PE. Transfer pricing is a key international tax issue for MNCs recognising that there is a clear connection between double taxation and transfer pricing. Global surveys indicate that 61% [1] of the MNCs consider transfer pricing as a key concern today and for years to come.

The concept of transfer pricing becomes relevant from the viewpoint of revenue authorities. Every jurisdiction would be interested in getting a fair share of revenue in respect of economic activities carried out therein. The transfer pricing seeks to achieve this. It is also relevant from the management viewpoint, for various reasons, including decision-making, evaluation of performance of the enterprise or a unit, and to arrive at fair profit of an enterprise.

Transfer pricing developed as a logical result of the movement towards divisionalisation of operations by large business organisations like General Motors and General Electric in US during the early part of the twentieth century. Highly centralised operations were decentralised by establishing numerous profit centres in search for more productivity. Delegation of increased authority to local managers in turn gave rise to a mechanism of internal pricing that would serve the dual purpose, on the one hand of optimising allocation of corporate resource, and on the other of motivating the divisional managers to operate their units at a high degree of efficiency so that goal congruence prevails between divisional and corporate management. At the same time, it serves as a device for monitoring the performance of divisional managers.

The Concept

A division, branch, department of any other component of an entity may transfer goods or services to other subdivisions of the same entity. Transfers may be of tangible property like raw material, unfinished components, ready to sell items or services like marketing and distribution and research and development. The amount used to record such transfers between divisions is known as transfer price. Horngren and Foster defined transfer price as "the price one segment of an organisation (subunit, department, division and so on) charges for a product or service supplied to another segment of the same organisation". [2] A slightly modified version of this definition would include inter-company transfers between affiliates.

Transfer price can also be defined as exchange value assigned to a product or service that one unit of an organisation provides to another unit of the same organisation. The transfer price is entered as a credit in the books of the supplier and as a debit in the books of the receiver. In this dissertation, the terms division, unit, affiliate, company and wherever appropriate, subsidiary have been used interchangeably.

The significance of transfer pricing for a firm depends to a large extent on the quantum of transactions amongst its different segments. Where interdivisional transfers are minimal, the transfer price has little impact on segmental performance or taxation. On the other hand, substantial interdivisional transfers can have a dramatic effect on the reported performance or international tax liability.

Unique Features

- **An Offshoot of Cost Accounting**

Transfer pricing is an offshoot of cost accounting. When the organisation grows in size, the centralised control becomes more difficult. To this end, any entities have decentralised their activities into autonomous divisions or subsidiaries. This process of decentralisation has resulted in financial benefit to the organisation as a whole because of delegation of authority at the divisional level provides an added incentive. At this stage, the idea of transfer pricing was introduced. The concept seemed to be a good financial tool until it was used to try to measure what the price of transfer should be.

- **Cost Allocation**

It is the price used for internal transfer of goods and services between divisions of a business enterprise. In a sense, all cost allocation is a form of transfer pricing. The basic purpose of transfer pricing is to allocate cost to the production department.

- **Critical Success Factor**

There are several financial and non-financial factors for a business to succeed. Variables are there which make things happen. Performance of any organisation has to be judged not simply in financial terms of net profit or its derivatives like Rate of Return on Investment (ROI) or Residual Income (RI). Research has rightly emphasised the significance of non-financial variables like customer satisfaction. Transfer pricing belongs to the area of financial factors. This is exactly what has been referred to as the "Balanced Scorecard". Any transfer pricing method has to get integrated. An integrated transfer pricing system should have been developed by the joint efforts of both accounting and manufacturing personnel. If a divisional manager is responsible for divisional performance, he should have had input in the development of transfer pricing system. Failure to follow this method will result in sub-optimisation of resource.

Mechanism of Transfer Pricing

Reinvoicing centres are set up in tax heavens. [3] They are used to coordinate transfer pricing around the world. Intercorporate transactions are routed through the reinvoicing centres. The reinvoicing centre takes title to the goods sold by the selling unit and results them to the receiving unit. The prices received by the seller and charged to the buyer are determined administratively. There is no interference with the actual flow of go0ods which are shipped from the seller to the buyer but the documentation show the two stage transfer. The purpose is to siphon the profits away from a high tax parent or affiliate to low tax affiliates and position funds in locations with strong currencies and virtually no exchange controls.

Requisites of an Optimal Method

A transfer pricing method should have the characteristics which make it an effective system. The criteria, which a good transfer pricing should satisfy, though not necessarily all are the following:

- **Objectively Determinable and Fair**

The system adopted must be fair to all the parties concerned; it must be objectively determinable and impartial to the event possible. It should not favour manager of one division against another. The inequalities in the system will cause its breakdown. It should minimise the conflict between buying and selling units. Conflicts over transfer pricing are inevitable but techniques should be developed to reduce internal differences and conflicts.

- **Goal Congruence**

The pricing system should be consistent with the overall corporate objectives. It should encourage managers to pursue corporate goals together with their persona goals; no decision should be permitted to act in a way that is in contradiction with comp-any objectives. The system ought to be designed to ensure that divisional management and top management would make the same optimal decision if all the information available is known to the parties. The method must promote cooperation across divisions.

- **Economic Efficiency**

The pricing system must promote utilisation of resources to achieve the maximum benefit possible. It should act as an incentive to keep costs down and facilitate sped and minimise delays. It must offer a fast response to changing business challenges in the world.

- **Simple and Flexible**

Then, the system has to be reasonably simple, minimising duplication and paper work. It must offer flexibility where and when it is needed.

- **Long Range in Scope**

The transfer pricing system should be long range in scope. It should not sub-optimise by pursuing only short-range objectives. Once long range perspective is lost track of, the system could be disastrous.

Governing Considerations

Transfer pricing technique is dependent on an industry's economic conditions, corporate return and sales policies. There are various considerations that may force multinationals to manipulate transfer pricing to their advantage. The factors that are likely to prompt transfer pricing are:

- **Coordinate and Control Operations**

Transfer pricing is one of the tools by which global resources can be controlled and allocated by the headquarter. Generally, the headquarters have access to the data base needed to make resource decisions in the long-term interest of the whole firm which may at times run counter to the short-run benefits of certain units or divisions. In such cases, the interest of the sub-unit must be coordinated to those of the whole firm. Transfer pricing serves as the core of the database used for decision making reports to the headquarter. It must reflect the relevant cost involved, regardless of the transfer pricing reflected in transactions among sub-units. Consequently, meaningful cost accumulations for internal reporting dictate that transfer of resources with the MNC is based upon cost.

- **Minimise Overall Corporation Tax on Profits**

Multinational corporations, like other companies try to maximise their profits, Corporation tax is an important variable in case of transfer pricing. Many companies try to increase their net world income by manoeuvring their profits to the lowest tax areas. If in country A, the corporation tax burden is higher than in country B, other circumstances being equal, the multinational is rewarded when it overprices its sales from B to A. The transfer pricing gambits are particularly profitable whenever tax rates in two countries diverge widely. Prof. J.S. Arpon, after analysing the transfer pricing policies of some 60 non-US multinational firms and their subsidiaries, found that French, Italian, Canadian and Ameŕican companies considered income tax to be the most important variable effecting transferring pricing policy. Other things being equal, profits accruing to the corporate system as a whole can be increased by setting a higher transfer price to siphon profits from subsidiaries domiciled in high tax countries and setting a low transfer price to subsidiaries located in low tax countries. As an example, Blue Jeans, Hong Kong, a wholly owned manufacturing subsidiary of Global Enterprises (U.S.A) ships 5,00,000 pairs of designer blue jeans to a related U.S. Sales affiliate, Blue Jeans – U.S.A. also wholly owned by Global Enterprises, for $6 a pair. Assuming wholesale price of each garment is $12 in the United States, consolidated profits (after eliminating inter company sales and costs) and taxes would total $11,44,000 and 7,56,000 respectively. This is shown in Table 1.1.

Given a US corporate tax rate of 46 per cent versus only 16.5 per cent in Hong Kong, an increase in the transfer price of Blue Jeans from $ 6 to $ 8.5 a pair produces a system which benefits as shown in Table 1.2.

Thus, we see that by raising the transfer price charged by Hong Kong affiliate, increases the taxable income there and

Table 1.1

Consolidated Profits from Blue Jeans

	Blue Jeans Hong Kong ($)	Blue Jeans U. S.A. ($)	Global Enterprises ($)
Sales	30,00,000	60,00,000	60,00,000
Cost of Sales	*21,00,000	**30,00,000	21,00,000
Gross Margin	9,00,000	30,00,000	39,00,000
Operating Expenses	5,00,000	15,00,000	20,00,000
Pre-tax Income	4,00,000	15,00,000	19,00,000
Income Tax (16.5 % / 46 %)	66,000	6,90,000	7,56,000
Net Income	3,34,000	8,10,000	11,44,000

* Equal to 70% of Sales

** Based on transfer price of $ 6 per unit.

Table – 1.2

Consolidated Profits from Blue Jeans with Transfer Price Increase

	Blue Jeans Hong Kong ($)	Blue Jeans U. S.A.($)	Global Enterprises ($)
Sales	42,50,000	60,00,000	60,00,000
Cost of Sales	21,00,000	42,50,000	21,00,000
Gross Margin	21,50,000	17,50,000	39,00,000
Operating Expenses	5,00,000	15,00,000	20,00,000
Pre-tax Income	16,50,000	2,50,000	19,00,000
Income Tax (16.5 % / 46 %)	2,72,250	1,15,000	3,87,250
Net Income	13,77,750	1,35,000	15,12,750

reduces taxable income for the U.S. affiliate by $12,50,000. Owing to the differential tax rate of 29.5 percent between U.S.A. and Hong Kong, corporate income taxes for the MNC as a whole decrease by 3,68,750 with an increase in consolidated after tax earnings.

- **Customs Duties**

  In another fiscal area of custom duties, transfer pricing manipulation can be expected to entail benefits to multinational corporations. Suppose, a commodity with a normal price of 1,000 is subjected to a 60 percent import duty in country M. It pays to the multinational to lower the value declared on the transaction to 700 as the import duty will be reduced by 180. These are differences between filed of corporate taxation and of import duties. In the area of custom duties, only value lowering transfer pricing tactics are profitable as regards corporate taxes, depending on the circumstances would involve under pricing or over charging the normal price. Also, when the multinational lowers the value declared on the commodities declared in country M, only that country is involved. The exporting country X would experience no gain or loss in customs revenues.

- **Competitive Variables**

  In order to facilitate the establishment of a subsidiary abroad, a parent company could supply the subsidiary with inputs invoiced at very low prices. The price subsidies would gradually be removed as the foreign affiliate strengthens its competitive foothold in the foreign market. Similarly, lower fashion prices could be used to shield an existing operation from the effects of increased foreign competition. Indirect competitive effects are also possible. In order to improve foreign subsidiary's access to local capital markets, its reported earnings and financial position can be bolstered by setting low transfer prices on the subsidiary's inputs and high transfer prices on its outputs.

- **Environmental Hazards**

  Risks associated with the overseas investments can also be reduced by selective use of the transfer price. A high transfer price can be used to return resources to the parent firm as soon as possible if the short-term investment is made or when the political environment is deteriorating and considered to be irreversible. Exchange risk is also one of the reasons for using the mechanism of transfer pricing. Floating-exchange-risk has made companies engaged in international trade and investment view exchange uncertainties as their most pervasive risk. Devaluation of currency involves not only monetary items such as cash, receivables but also real assets like real estate.

- **Profit and Capital Repatriation**

Governments of all countries impose restrictions on repatriation of profits and capital. Thus, foreign exchange control is quite stringent particularly in developing countries where situation of balance of payments is very tight. MNCs view stringent restrictions on profit remittances as negative parameters on their profit and sales maximisation. Transfer pricing manipulation can circumvent the explicit restrictions on the remittances, e.g., the prices of sales by the parent to the subsidiary are artificially raised. Conversely, sales of the latter are under priced. Such a device substitutes the direct dividend route. Thus, the objectives of transfer pricing vary. The relative significance of these depends on the quantum of transactions between its different segments. Of late, exchange control and profit repatriation has kept precedence over minimising tax liability as the object of transfer pricing.

Transfer Pricing in Conglomerates and Multinationals in India

In fact, the subject of transfer pricing has failed to attract the attention of people in India. So far, limited research has been undertaken on this issue. The primary constraint is lack of willingness on the part of companies to disclose the required information. In an earlier study, Govindrajan and Ramamurthy [4] concluded that market price based transfers were popular wit companies in India. This was followed by manufacturing cost-based prices. However, a recent study by Shirin Rathore [5] reveals that other methods such as sales minus and negotiated price methods are gaining ground probably on account of their ability to achieve better the objectives of transfer pricing.

Transfer price mechanism employed by multinationals and conglomerates has been an olive-green area of interest of management accountants and high echelons of management. It is a major policy decision and requires several inputs. The present book entails to study various transfer pricing methods in the used by conglomerates and multinationals in India. With this underlying objective, the book focuses on:

(1) background and nuisances of the available methods.

(2) assessing the developments in the legislation and standards related to transfer pricing in developed countries,

(3) evaluating the transfer pricing policy in India as also to look into implications of the recent enactments in India,

(4) few case studies about transfer pricing in India.

Notes

1. Ernst and Young, Global Transfer Pricing Survey, 1999.
2. Horngren C.T., and Foster, G., "Cost Accounting: A Managerial Emphasis", 7th Edition, Prentice-Hall of India, New Delhi, 1991, Chapter 22.
3. R.L. Varshney, S. Bhashyam, "International Financial Management – An Indian Perspective".
4. Govindrajan, V. and Ramamurthy, B., *Transfer Pricing Policies in Indian Companies*, "The Chartered Accountant", Nov., 1983, pp 296 – 301.
5. Rathore, Shri, *Transfer Pricing - Emerging Dimensions*, "Management Accounting", Vol. 34 00, 26-31.

2

Multinational Corporations – Goals and National Interests

The rise of multinational enterprises has been one of the most remarkable phenomenon in past world war period. These are defined as firms, which carry production and distribution activities in more than one country. These are big and dynamic enterprises with operations in many product lines and in many countries. Their activities are globally coordinated by groups of persons, exercising tight control on men, money and markets. They derive strength from their vast capital, sophisticated technology, and brand names. At present, there are probably more than 63,000 corporations in the world, which are called multinational and multi-locational firms or which are popularly known as multinational corporations.

Introduction

There is neither a universally accepted definition of a multinational corporation nor of the words 'international' and 'transnational', which are also widely used. [1] The term 'multinational corporation' is often taken as the synonym of 'transnational corporation' and recently the United Nations has renamed 'multinationals' as 'transnationals'. In many instances, an international enterprise is taken as synonym of the widely used American term 'multinational corporation' [2]. Several scholars have classified the 'multinational corporations' according to their geographical location or spread (international, transnational, multinational and supernational), function [3] (colonial companies, resource based companies, public utility companies, manufacturing companies and service companies), and motivation [4] (ethnocentric, polycentric and geocentric). In spite of an overall similarity between the terms used to denote multinational corporations, there are subtle differences between the terms. The organisation termed as 'international' means an organisation which engages in foreign trade but without enormous investment in the participating countries. The organisation categorised as the 'transnational' represents a stage wherein ownership and control of the concerned organisation crosses national boundaries. Hence, a multinational company may be called 'transnational' or 'international' but a 'transnational' (company which crosses only national boundary in ownership and control) or international company (the company which engages in trade across the national boundary but without enormous investment in participating countries) cannot be the synonym with multinational.

Structure and Formation

As stated above, the multinational corporations are large companies having enormous resources - financial, technical and managerial. The natural question arises, how do they become large? In this respect, it may be noted that because any private sector or public sector enterprise cannot invest in different countries at once, the companies which emerge, as multinationals become large either through merger of a number of companies or through establishing subsidiaries in other countries.

Figure 2.1 attempts to understand the formation of a multinational company on the basis of merger of number of companies. There are a number of companies (X1, X2, X3, X4...XN) operating in different countries. Suppose companies namely X4 and X5 merge and similarly companies namely X6 and X7 get merged, they would emerge as companies X45 and X67 respectively. Similarly, merger of company X3 and X45 and X8 and X67 would give rise to company X345 and X678 respectively. Thus, merger of companies X1 and X2 to company X345 and X9 and Xn to company X678 would help emergence of companies namely X12345 and X6789...n respectively. And these two major companies (X12345 and X6789... n) can further unite to form X1...n. The company X...n therefore, will, no doubt be, a large company and operating functions (manufacture, distribution,

Figure 2.1: Formation of Multinational Company Type - 1

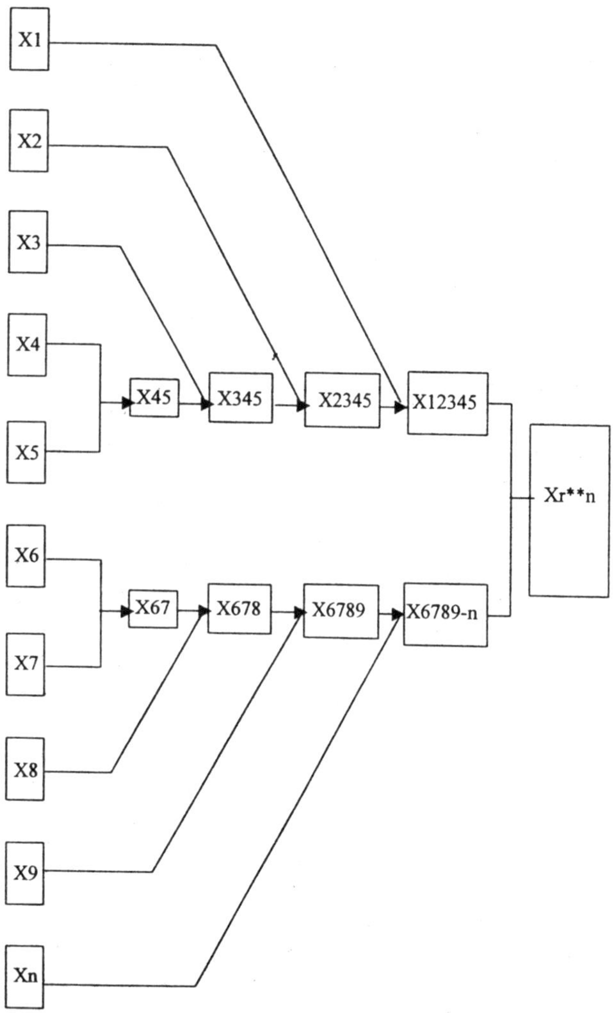

finance and sale), among several nations. Its investments and profits will also be large but merger materialises only if the bidder believes that he can make a better use of assets of the concerned companies than the existing individual managements or if all the participants agree that their combined forces would be stronger for better growth and profitability than should they remain apart.

The British Leyland Motor Corporation (merger of 10 companies), International Computers (merger of 9 companies), the French Electrical Industry (merger of 8 companies) are some of the important examples of the merger. In the area of transnational merger, the names of Shell and Unilever merit special attention and they in fact initiated formation of multinationals through the ground of merger.

The other method of formation of multinational corporations is by opening its subsidiaries in a number of countries. This case is understood by Figure 2.2. Suppose a company (parent company) having established its subsidiary in country, A, expands its business through establishing its subsidiaries in countries B, C, D, and n respectively and exercises control over these companies. A company turns into a multinational corporation when the companies in country A, B, C, D and n mature and again open their subsidiaries in A1, A2...An countries and similarly B1, B2...Nn; C1, C2...Cn; D1, D2...Dn and finally N1, N2...Nn and also exercising control on these subsidiaries. Thus, the parent company will be a large company having higher investment and management potential, for example, Seimen Co. (India) Ltd., Boots Co. (India) Ltd., etc.

The method of specific formation of a company gives rise to the structure of a company. Whether a parent company opens its subsidiary or it merges with other companies, depends to a large extent upon its strategic planning system and financial base. There are various orgnisational structures classified by Dereck F. Channon [5], but there is no clear and correct choice with respect to appropriate organisational structure that a firm should adopt at any particular point in its strategic development. Some clear patterns however, do emerge but the choice of organisational

Figure 2.2: Formation of Multinational Company Type - 2

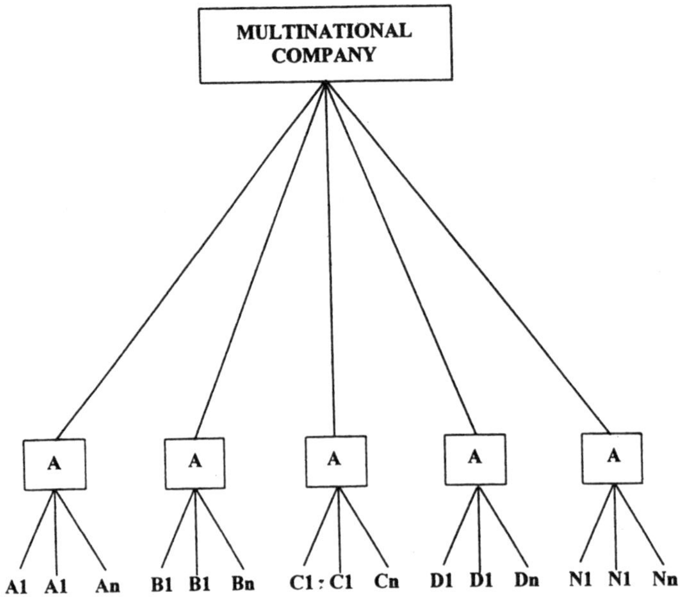

structures adopted by the multinational enterprise is an essential feature underlying its development in overseas markets. The choice of structure has a significant effect on the choice of internal planning system because the transnational merger can play a dramatic role in shaping the organisational structure, for example, Japanese Ziabatsu [6] Structure. The structure of the Japanese Zaibatsu is shown for the clear understanding of the functioning of its specific structure (Figure 2.3). Its linkages have extended transnationally and, therefore, quite ready to form joint ventures in response to the local government. The central trading company acts as an intelligence centre. It collects information from around the world on market trends and identifies new growth opportunities. Organisational structure, thus, depends on a company's planning.

Multinationals – Role and Significance

Multinational enterprises have attained their present dominant economic position through a long process of growth. Many of them started as small workshops and factories in the late eighteenth or early nineteenth century. Advantage of scientific discoveries by incorporating technological changes in their production operation, expanded on the national scale by mobilising internal profits as well as external sources of finance, professionalizing the management of their expanding division in several regions and ultimately encompassed almost the entire globe with their products and ideas. Accelerating concentration of industry and banking with multinationalisation of their operations is the hallmark of the process of growth. In order to avoid inefficiency and streamline growth, the multinational corporations have evolved a well-integrated organisational system through inter-corporate and inter-country block holding. In order to expand their business abroad they provide financial support to political parties and thereby exercise influence on government policies wherever they operate. They also get a certain amount of support and political protection from the government of their base countries. The support in the form of tax concessions, diplomatic

Figure 2.3: Scheme of Zaibatsu Structure Including International Linkages

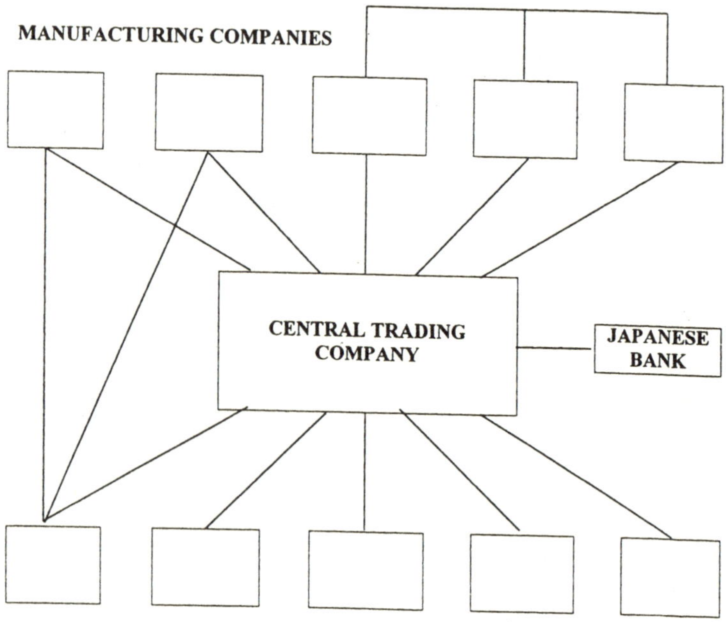

Foreign Manufacturing Companies Jointly Owned By Japanese Companies And Local Interest

Source : Vernon, R. and Wells, L. The Manager in the International Economy (Prentice Hall, Third Edition), N.J., 1976, p. 32.

clout and preferential access to government controls strengthens the economic base of the corporations.

The control of technology by the world's top 200 industrial corporations, of finance by the top twenty banks and of the instruments of developing and disseminating information and ideology by the largest advertising agencies. They have undermined the traditional rule of national and international institutions and free market in determining the allocation resources. These enterprises have grown bigger even than the national states, their operations have become more powerful than national policies and their organisational network has made the existing institutional framework obsolete.

The multinational corporate systems affect the world society in more than one ways. It influences the society's major economic decisions namely, what to produce, how much to produce, where to produce and how to produce (which technology to use). These decisions determine the use of world's resources and the distribution of world production, and thereby the current and future control on resource. It is clear that the development of this system to date has served the interests of only a few, while the majority of world's citizens are deprived of even the bare necessities of life.

Several attempts have been made to understand the process of development of multinationals, and the implications of this process in the growth of society in general and capitalism in particular. These studies can broadly be classified into two categories: those supporting the expansion of the multinational corporations wholly or partially, and those critical of their current role.

Goals of Multinationals

The primary goal of multinationals is the growth, profitability and efficiency. Their sole objective is profit maximisation. To achieve profitable growth, the multinationals stress the efficient use of resources, human, material, energy, land and capital, [7] by using various strategies for achieving growth and profitability as product innovation, market segmentation, improved services, etc. These strategies help developing countries achieve the goal of efficiency to increase productivity, which is directly related with goal of growth and profit maximisation.

The secondary goal of multinationals is the 'global rationalisation'. As they have capacity to allocate production across countries, a multinational company by definition can equalise to some extent the cost of capital across national lines.

The goal of multinational corporations appears in three states in respect of developing countries. In the first stage, developing countries as the source of raw materials, in the later stage as the bases for internal market and in the last stage, as the bases for external markets. Thus, these goals turn about to the decision to invest, the utilization of appropriate technology and production method, environmental acceptability, plan location, control of financial business and technology practices and personal policies of parents and subsidiaries.

Practically, the goals of multinational corporations and the host governments differ which leads to conflict between the two. The goal of a corporation concentrates largely on growth and profit, while that of the host government on growth with welfare. The case of home country controls over multinational firms are not related to the good or bad intention nor does it have to rest on charges of 'abuses' or 'exploitation' by multinational companies but actually the goal of the host country and the parent country is not identical. The multinational enterprise attempts to direct as corporate family of diverse nationalities under its control towards supranational goals. Each member of the parent has some national sentiments and a group of members operates as a transnational system that rationalises its business goal on global basis and the goals among the different groups may be the similar or contrasting. If their goals differ, the conflicts arise with their goals of national state. Each multinational enterprise tries to maximise its national goals (due to nationalistic sentiments). Hence potential conflict arises between the multinational enterprise and the national state. There is no basic conflict between the multinational company's goal of maximising profits in each country and overall profit maximisation stated by Jacoby. [8] According to him, to maximise global profit, a multinational enterprise will use transfer pricing and other strategies to position profits in those countries wit the lowest tax rates and this makes conflicts in each country of operations. Kindleberger [9] has defined international corporation / Label Multinational which is willing to speculate against the currency of the head office because it regards holding of cash anywhere as subject to exchange risk which should be hedged.

Development Theories

Foreign direct investment plays in important role to break the vicious circle in developing countries. Development is constrained by shortage of foreign exchange in the standard two-gap models. [10] Foreign direct investment fulfils the goals of efficiency and growth because it pursues the highest rate of available return, which increases world welfare. The market allocates the benefits of foreign investments, some of which are bound to accrue to the host country. [11] Technology too brings the structural change in country's developmental process. The modern economic theory of development regards technical progress as the most crucial factor explaining structural changes and economic growth. [12] Technology narrows the gap between developed and developing nations. Developing countries are the 'late comers' and have wider range and more choice for accessed to technology than developed countries. Development in the last 100 years in Japan and Canada proves this clearly. In the beginning, Japan imported a very small sum of infrastructure investment and without restraint technology with a very high multiplier impact. Canada collected domestic capital to use in infrastructure investment such as rail, road, health care, etc. with a very high multiplier effect. Foreign capital channelled for manufacturing and mining led to a very rapid development within less than two decades.

Product cycle theory as stated by Raymond and Vernon [13] explain three phases of the cycle. The first phase explains creation of product through technological innovation. In the second phase diffusion of technology takes place and third phase of the theory is related to export of component or finished product of the subsidiary. In other words, Vernon's product cycle theory asserts that process technologies diffuse as products get better established and ultimately when product get matured, the transferability of various other elements of technology increases. The lower unit cost of production advantages enables less developed countries (LDCs) to seek transfer of technology. [14] Thus, the theory provides a cycle; a continuous innovation which narrows the gap [15] between the LDCs and the under developed countries (UDCs). Hence, it is the extension of Schumpetarian theory of development and it has been hypothesized that in the last phase of product cycle, MNCs find it profitable to transfer technologies, either to their own subsidiary or through licensing agreements to LDCs. [16]

The proponent of Raymond Vernon's product cycle approach viewed its implications for development while industrial economists asserted that the direct foreign investment wad dominated by oligopolistic industries. So the prosecutor of latter's theory negated to conventional theory that investment will take place where returns are the highest. Thus, controversies between two schools of economists are the problem of third world and it has created a dilemma.

The school of thought, which emphasises the positive role of multinationals, consists of two groups of writers. One group considers multinationals the paragon of all virtues and, therefore, would like to provide an unrestricted environment for their growth. This group is pure, global neoclassical school, (Business Week) 1970, Ford, 1971, and Freeman 1976) which believes in the efficacy of market mechanism to achieve a fully rational international division of labour. They regard the multinationals as the workhorses of the world, the mighty engines of enlightened capitalism, agent of worldwide Pareto-optimality leading to optimum use of world's productive resources and a genuine vehicle of international cooperation. According to their view restrictions on the activities, of MNCs by nation states would result in suboptimal utilisation of the world's resources. Therefore, they suggest that the MNCs should be given a free hand to harness these resources in any country of the world.

The second group, moderate in tone, is typified by Vernon (1971 and 1977), Dunning (1970 and 1972), and Rofle (1969). They trace the expansion of multinationals to three non-political trends, (i) decline in the cost of international transportation (ii) decline in the cost of international communication, and (iii) rise in the cost of generating and launching major industrial innovations. These conditions underline the efficiency o the multinational. They further, point out that these multinationals are forced to disassociate themselves from the political and economic objectives of both home and host countries because that would presumably ensure their business credibility in several count5ies with diverse political environment. MNCs generate costs as well as benefits to parent country and to the host country. Benefits accrue to the parent country in the form of repatriated profits, linked exports orders and competitive advantages in the world markets and cost have to be incurred in terms of outflow of funds, transfer of production and consequent loss of potential employment to the host country.

MNCs provide a package of new products, technology, capital and management skills which contribute to national economic welfare but they also undermine the growth of domestic industries and purse certain productive activities which are counter to the national interest. The calculation of these costs and benefit has been suggested to evaluate the role of MNCs. A country should invite those multinationals, which offer benefits greater than the cost. In the cases where nation states have weaker bargaining power than that of multinationals, some regulation of MNCs by supra-national institution is justified. Less developed countries can interfere with world market forces for the reasons of protecting 'infant industries' but they are nevertheless cautioned against impossible attempts to do without multinationals.

The Critics' View of Multinationals

The critics' view of MNCs can also be arranged in two groups: The radical economists like Barnet and Muller (1975), Mandel (1969, 1970), Murray (1971) and Rowthorn (1971), etc. and the explicitly Marxists typified by Sweezy (1978, 1979), Megdoff (1969, 1978, 1979), Hymmer (1972, 1978) and Krosigk (1972). The radical economists point out the multinationals derive high profit on the basis of oligopolistic control of domestic and foreign market and the growth of multinationals supported by high profit, in turn, enables them to exercise still greater power in foreign markets. As multinationals grow, they also undermine the political power of the nation state. Thus, the oligopolistic nature of international business is a necessary cause and an effect of a world-wide hierarchy of economic dependence power and welfare Radica H (1975 p.12).

Furthermore, Barnet and Muller point out that multinational corporations have a disruptive impact on the international economic and the political system.

(1) Multinationals convert a large proportion of international trade into intra company trade (between affiliates o the same company).

(2) They control a significant international floor of money through unrecorded transactions.

(3) They deny to even the largest countries, Germany and United States, the economic tools to restore stability and create antagonism between developed and under developed countries and between the rich and the poor everywhere. In short they act as disturbers of the peace on a global scale. According to the radical economists, therefore, the activities of MNCs require rigorous control to maintain a stable relationship with the nation-state.

The Marxist View

Marxists consider the multinationals basic institutional forms of the capitalist world economy in its neo-imperialist state. According to the Marxists the only solution to the contradictions of capitalism unleashed by MNCs is to develop a strong international working class movement.

Growth of Multinationals

It should be mentioned at the outset that barring a few exceptions, MNCs are multinational in operation and not in ownership and management. Professor Vernon points out that 65 per cent (or 3730 out of 5727) subsidiaries of the top 180 U.S. based multinationals were wholly owned by their parents and 21.4 per cent were majority owner (with 50 per cent or more share held by their parents); the top 135 Europe and U.K. based enterprises and 72.5 per cent (2612 out of 3503) subsidiaries as wholly owned.

Thus, the multinational enterprise is as 'multinational' as the Indian army was 'Indian' under the British Raj; while the troops were Indians, the officer was British.

There 63,000 multinationals, with more than 900,000 affiliates worldwide. Their revenue represents approximately one-tenth of the world's gross domestic product (GDP). 90 percent of the top 100 are located in the European Union, United States, and Japan. These multinationals are large in terms of both production and assets. Their immense economic power is indicated by the fact that some of them produce more than the gross national products of medium sized countries.

To take a few examples, American Telephone and Telegraph produces more than do the entire economies of Greece, Israel, Norway and Venezuela, General Motors produces more than do the national economies of either New Zealand or Pakistan, Royal Dutch shell is bigger than Iran, Venezuela and Turkey; and the Chrysler is bigger than Ethiopia.

Need for Inviting Multinationals

The multinationals are economically important institutions for developing countries because the latter needs both foreign exchange earning and facilities for greater production. The developing countries have more capital than they can productively employ. Multinationals help them increase their productivity by optimum mobilization of resources: human, capital or physical, through transfer of technology and direct foreign investment. It may be mentioned that for the developing countries, appropriate technology and even a small sum of foreign capital can have a significant multiplier impact. The multinationals have the ability to integrate and allocate the productive resources on global basis in the best interest of the developing nations. The need for inviting multinationals (MNCs) would help create employment and reduce burden of foreign exchange through import substitution and setting up labour intensive industries, etc.

The bad repute or MNCs may be holding the rate of spread of multinationals into the developing world below the ideal rate. [17]

The direct foreign investment increases the capital stock, productive capacity, technical know-how and managerial skill in the host country. Multinational corporations accomplish the transfer of technology by direct operational contact between worker and technology by sending blue prints etc. but it was expected by the foreign subsidiaries to contribute to net capital formation through reinvestment of its profits. If the profits are siphoned off to the parent corporation the rate of reinvestment will be unacceptably low.

MNCs are also criticized for their activities of neo-colonialism. MNCs serve as the connecting link between production in the developing nations and the market for primary products in the developed world. [18] There are some examples in which multinationals are larger than the host country's economies. In such cases, the ability to negotiate is unequal and the large MNC has a decisive advantage. The existence of large number of MNCs can lead to a significant proportion of relatively technologically advanced sector in developing nations and thus these nations being under the control of foreigners. When the host country's executives are not indigenous people, the country does not have power over its own economy and the formation of national economic goal is exercise in frustration. [19]

In dependencia literature, it has been aptly remarked that (a) host country receive too few benefits; (b) that foreign investment causes distortions in the local economies, and (c) that foreign-investment distorts 'host country' political process. [20]

Dependencia proposition states, the benefits of foreign investment are 'poorly' (or 'unfairly' or 'unequally') distributed between multinational, and the host country pays 'too high' a price for what it gets, or the company siphons off an economic 'surplus' that could otherwise be used to finance internal development. [21]

The usual means of siphon off profits to the parent is by means of transfer pricing, exports at less than world price and invoicing imports from the parent corporation at some excessive profit rate of mark-up. S second source of inadequate performance is to be seen when the MNC subsidiary managers to earn a pure economic rent on a natural resource so that the contribution of the subsidiary to GDP (Gross Domestic Product) is very small. Another source of profit of parent countries is through royalties fess and services, managerial fees, transfer pricing and tax structure etc. Host countries are not able to afford the supply of such a large amount of foreign exchange. And also multinational corporations are not entitled to take undue advantage of their organisational form to escape from those conditions, which the host government imposes, on indigenous firm. [22]

The MNCs' subsidiaries shall identify the need for improved flows of foreign exchange and shall be sensitive to the host government legitimate concern. Hymer, Kindleberger, Wells, Stobaugh, Vernon and others [23] – developed the theory of oligopolistic expansion – and predicted that dependentistas asserts the question of 'proper price' to be paid to foreign investors by the host countries. As Kindleberger have stated the idea of upper and lower limits of the price that would have to be paid to the foreign investors and the actual price paid to the foreign investor, would be a function of relative bargaining strength of two sides. [24] Certainly, it is possible that the physical existence of the MNC in a nation and the national development of the host will combine to shift the bargaining strength in favour of the host. The relative bargaining strengths are likely to change over time in favour of the host government. But once the MNCs are established, they cannot be eliminated easily. [25]

Bargaining capability means little if it is not exercised for political reasons [26] but it has been seen that political interference suppress the actual benefit of inviting multinational corporations and this factor dominates over the other positive effects of direct foreign investment and transfer of technologies which abolishes the actual goal of multinational corporation and turn into an exploiting organisation whose aim is profit maximisation and access of natural resources from poor countries.

Regulations and Control

Each multinational buying or investing company is bound to certain guidelines formed by both the parties host and the parent government and these guidelines are mostly in favour of parent companies because they have more bargaining strength and monopoly power than developing countries. Due to these constraints, host country is not able to get benefits of foreign investments. Parent countries impose certain entry barriers for investment as well as for entry into world markets. Besides this, restrictions on trade marks, brand name and production pattern, payment of minimum royalty, post termination restrictions, use of expatriate persons and discouragement of local research and development are also imposed. Foreign Exchange Regulation Act (FERA) has restricted the production of certain commodities. Often parent country imposes variety of conditions which limit the dynamic effects of transfer of technologies. Some technologies are available only on payment of a considerable sum of money or the temporary monopoly power granted to the patent holder – imposes restrictions on competitive entry into the world market and may force buyer to import raw materials and intermediate machinery and equipment from particular source only. [27]

The number of restrictive business practices in developing countries exercise considerable adverse impact on trade and development in developing countries. The business practices may be classified under five heads, [28] as: (a) Restrictive business practices in patent licensing arrangements, (b) Restrictive business practices in know-how arrangements, (c) Restrictive business practices in trade mark licensing arrangements, and (d) Restrictive business practices – common to patents, know-how and trade mark licensing arrangements and (e) Insertion of 'most favoured license' clause in licensing contact are the most effective form of restrictive business practices as reported by developing countries. [29] Other restrictive practices related to patents, know how and trade mark licensing arrangements may be stated as: tied purchase of raw material and equipments of the licensee or any other person approved by him, compulsory acceptance of additional patents or know-how not required by the license, high royalties on goods produced for export purposes, fixing prices of products manufactured by the license, obtaining patens or know how or trade marks from other licensee with regard to the sale or manufacture of competing products and the obligation to use the distribution channels of licensee.

In addition to the above, certain other restrictions, which have direct or indirect impact on both trade and development, [30] are explained below.

First, the multinational corporation decides the territorial and production allocation arrangements, nature of the product processed or the quantity of the products to be catered without regard even to the interest of developing countries.

Secondly, pricing policy of the multinational corporation affects developing countries by affecting the prices of inputs and outputs between subsidiary and parent company. It has far reaching effect on balance of payment position of the host country. And also the pricing policy of final product in host country may be used as weapon to discourage prospective entrants to the market.

Thirdly, transfer pricing acts as an advantageous source for the multinational corporations through movement of funds from developing countries to developed countries. It acts as a restrictive business practices because it affects competition at home and abroad and the manipulation in its transfer pricing, royalty charges, technical know-how, fees, payments for research and development affects global interest. The head office charges have dominant position while fixing prices by the multinational corporation.

Lastly, merger or takeover involving the multinational corporations may hit the interests of subsidiaries of foreign affiliates. The adverse effect on subsidiaries, certainly affects the economic structure of the developing country.

Social restrictions are also posed by developing and developed countries because the policy of production and distribution are mostly favourably inclined towards parent countries while taste and preferences differ in different developing/developed countries and this makes a source of conflict because of several reasons. First, the capital-intensive technologies are generally opposed by labour unions in developing countries because it may create unemployment in developing countries. Secondly, the cost of sophisticated technologies is high. So this technology does not suit according to the developing countries needs/taste and preference. Thus, the social tension exists on account of class, caste, racial, regional or lingual conflicts. Thirdly, the creation of two classes in industrial workers of the developing countries consequents to the entry to the multinational corporations makes a source of conflicts due to the creation of low-income earners in local industries and the high-income earners in the MNCs. Fourthly, the adoption of multinationals and the host countries' policies and practices that are much different to that of national customs and patterns'. [31]

The transnational corporations always transplant their cultural values in social values of the developing nations. These corporations are adopting number of ways to weaken or neutralize the collective bargaining strength of developing countries by the threat, centering their aim on shutting down a plant or transferring productive operations from one country to another. [32] Fifthly, the privileged position of the expatriate staff to local staffs and disparities in income perks and living conditions are also an area of conflict. Finally, the maladjustment to local environment led to a number of conflicts between the workers and the management e.g. Chrysler (Co.) in U.K., General Motors in Canada [33] and John Deenalanz A.G in Federal Republic of Germany. American firms generally operate on the basis of values and assumptions, which prove conflicting in their own country with that of local country.

Political interferences have also empowered multinationals to dominate economically in the host country. There is fundamental difference in the production and distribution pattern of the corporations and the government due to growth and profit bearing goal of the former and growth with welfare of the later, within the broader framework of the national policy. Hence, the objectives of the corporation and the Government clashes. The pursuance of the broader national policy may sacrifice the growth aspect of the development for the short period of time. The policy of a corporation and more specially the multinational corporation is not related with the development growth of a particular country but with their goal of growth and profit of the individual affiliates operating in the different countries of the world in pursuance of their global strategy. There are many instances which reveal that many public sector undertakings are incurring losses and are allowed to continue their functioning because their aim is to achieve their goal of welfare aspects as social equality by decentralisation and equal distribution of income and wealth.

The policy of Government always obstructs the pursuance of the nations while that of corporation is to subvert and disrupt the government's trade, fiscal or monetary policies through subversion of political influence in the top of hierarchy of government.

Impact of MNCs on the National Economy

The capacity of multinational corporations (MNCs) to circumvent or subvert the national politics [34] and programmes has resulted in the increased modern means of communication, new technological skill and capital, liberalised trade agreements, the general agreements on tariff and trade, the policy to integrate and centralise the production and trade strategy on a global scale, the capacity to bargain with the nation state on a global basis of agreements, patent rights, licenses and also the capacity to execute to cartel agreements with other concerns. Lockheed scandal has also exposed the role of multinationals in influencing the government decision. They can go to the extent of bribing diplomats, ministers and the policy makers in different countries of the world.

Thus, the concentration of economic power in the hands of few, the inequality of distribution of profits/benefits among different groups, the extinction of competition in the home market, the social inequalities and the tactics of transfer pricing adopted by various multinationals have generally effect contrary to the national policies persuaded by the Governments of the host countries.

On the mater of its impact on employment, multinationals have a tremendous capacity to create job on the one hand and it may realise job crises on the other hand (particularly) in developing worlds. The subsidiaries of MNC in developing worlds must oblige to use the labour intensive techniques, which they usually avoid.

On the issues relating impact of transfer of technology on developing countries, when it is transferred in term of managerial skill, know-how, patent, licensing and other technical information. No doubt, it increases technical capability but it has certain drawbacks also. Firstly, its economic cost is too high and secondly, they do not know what price they are paying for the transfer of technology. Besides, it affects employment, economic equality and product mix also.

The multinationals are large companies having enormous resources (managerial, technical and financial). Due to the large resources they exercise monopoly power on developing nations and instead of increasing developing countries welfare, they increase their own profit, mainly because members of multinational corporations are guided by nationalistic sentiments. For developing countries, the invitation to multinational corporations is necessary because appropriate technology and a small sum of foreign capital can have a multiplier effect on development of LDCs.

Conglomerates

A conglomerate [35] is a multi-firm organisation dealing in different activities and different markets. The scope of the activities of the several firms under a conglomerate set up could indeed be very large ranging from firms that merely speculate in the share market to firms that produce capital goods. However, it is desirable to classify the activities of the firm under a given conglomerate into broad groups such as finance and investment firms, trade and commercial firms and producing firms. Even the numerous producing firms could be operating in a wide variety of products from consumer goods to capital goods. The different market where the firms operate could be competitive, oligopolistic or purely monopolistic.

While the theory of the firm is well developed and has been more or less accepted, the theory of the multi-firm conglomerate hardly exists. IN fact, in India there has been no agreement even on the definition and existence of conglomerates. Here the conglomerates themselves are referred to as industrial houses. The Monopolies Inquiry Commission (MIC) in its report (1965) has identified the important industrial houses and the companies under each house. Some of the houses have disputed the number of companies that have been included under their umbrella. Very little information exists on the structure of the conglomerates whether it be relating to independence of the firm, their inter-relationship or to the nature of the apex authority.

Conclusion

The multinational corporations have come to occupy an increasingly important position in the economic, social and political affairs of the cotemporary world. The phrases nation wide operation, national company and national market, which once projected the ultimate in corporate success, no longer denote such eminence in the economic world, nor do they describe the ultimate goal, the apex of accomplishment, to the leaders of business. The horizons for business growth have receded, the scope of activities expanded, and the dimensions of the firm multiplied. International, transnational and multinational are the new magic words, the modern slogans for stature, importance and achievement.

Multinational enterprises have attained their present dominant economic position through a long process of growth. They have undermined the traditional role of national and international institutions and free market in determining the allocation of resources. These enterprises have grown bigger than even the nation-states, their operations have become more powerful than national policies and their organisational network has made existing institutional framework ineffective and obsolete. The multinational corporate system affects the world society in several ways. It influences the society's major economic decision namely, what to produce, how much to produce, where to produce and how to produce (which technology to use). These decisions determine the use of world resources and the distribution of world production, and thereby the current and future control on resources. To sum up, multinationals exercise decisive influence over the worldwide production and distribution and social relations by controlling technology, finance capital, and marketing network – three basic components of the corporate power.

Notes

1. Tugendhat, Christopher, "The Multinational", published by Penguin Books (Paper Back), 1974.
2. Livingstone, James: "The International Enterprise", Associated Business Programme, London, 1975.
3. Kolde, Endel Jacob: "The Multinational Corporation and Economic Growth", Economic Impact, No. 20, American Center, New Delhi.
4. Manser, WAP: "The Financial Role of Multinational Enterprise", Associated Business Programme, London, 1974.
5. Channon, Dereck F. and Jalland Michael, "Multinational Strategic Planning", Manchester Business School, 1976.

6. Vernon R. and Wells, L; "The Manager in the International Economy", (Prentice Hall, N.J. third edition), 1976, p.32.
7. Laszlo, Ervin et al., "Goals of Multinational Corporations", excerpts from Goals of Mankind, Research Foundation, State University of New York.
8. Jacoby, Neil, "Corporate Power and Social Responsibility", Macmillan, New Delhi, 1973, p.13.
9. Kindleberger, Charles P, "American Business Abroad", Yale University Press, New Haven (Conn.) 1969, p. 182.
10. Chenery, H. and Stout A, "Foreign Assistance and Economic Development", American Economic Review, Vol. LVI, Sept. 1966.
11. Mac Dougall, G.D.A., "The Benefits and Costs of Private Investment Abroad: A Theoretical Approach", Economic Record, March, 1960.
12. Schmookler I, 'Technical Change and Economic Theory", American Economic Review, X 102, Vol. LVPP 333, 1965, Solor R, "The Meaning and Measure of Economic Progress", Technology and Culture, Vol. 9, No. 31968, Quinn, J.S., "Technology Transfer by MNC", Business Review, Nov.-Dec. 1969.
13. Vernon, R., "International Investment in International Trade in Product Cycle", Quarterly Journal of Economics, May 1966.
14. Hirch, S, cited by Cooper, C. "Transfer of Technology to Latin America", Study of Science Policy Research Unit, Sussex University, 1970.
15. Poshner, M.V., "International Trade and Technical Change", Oxford Economic Papers, XIII, 1961: Mmenta J., "Economic Theory and Transfer of Technology", Proceedings of a Conference on Transfer of Technology to LDCs, April 1966.
16. Clark N, "The Multinational Corporation: The Transfer of Technology and Dependence", Development and Change, Vol. VI, No. 1975, pp.6-8.
17. Gray, Peter H, "Gains from Hosting Multinationals: A Reassessment", Douglass College, Rutgers University (mimeographed). He stated that there is, of course, no way of measuring the ideal rate but such knowledge, ideological differences with respect to virtues of public and private ownership of the means of production also affect the spread of MNCs.
18. Akin L, Mobounge, "International Circumstances Affecting the Development and Trade of Developing Countries", in Bertil Ohlin

et al. (eds.). The International Allocation of Economic Activity, Macmillan Press, London, 1977, pp 432-447.

19. Gray and Gail, E. Makinen, "The Balance of Payments Contributions of Multinational Corporations", Journal of Business, (July 1967), pp 339-43.
20. Frank, Andre Gunder, "Capitalism and Under Development in Latin America: Historical Studies of Chile and Brazil", Monthly Review Press, New York, 1969, also Bodenheimer, S. "Dependency and Imperialism: The Roots of Latin American Underdevelopment" in K. Fann and Hodges (eds) Reading in U.S. Imperialism, Proter Sargent, Boston, 1971.
21. Moran, Theodore H., "Multinational Corporations and Dependency: A Dialogue for Dependentistas and Non-dependentistas", International Organisation, Winter, 1978.
22. Hawkins, Robert G. and Donald Macaluso, "The Avoidance of Restrictive Policies in Host Countries by Multinational Firms", Journal of Money Credit and Banking, November, 1977, pp-562-571.
23. Hymer, Stephen, "The International Operations of National Film: A Study of Direct Investment", (Ph. D dissertation) Massachusetts Institute of Technology, 1960; Kindleberger, C.P. American Business Abroad: Six Lectures on Direct Investment, Yale University Press, New Haven, Com: 1969, Vernon, Raymond, 196, op. cit., Sovereignty at Bay: "The Multinational Spread of U.S. Enterprises", Basic Books, New York, 1971, Stobaugh, Robert, B. The Product Life Cycle, US Exports and International Investment, (Ph. D dissertation), Harvard Business School, 1968).
24. Penrose T., "Profit Sharing between Producing Countries and Oil Companies in Middle East", Economic Journal, 1959. Kindleberger C.P., "Economic Development", McGraw Hill, New York, 2nd ed., 1965, p.334.
25. Kindleberger, C.P. and Henick, Bruce, "Economic Development", 3rd Edition, McGraw Hill, New York, 1977, p.320.
26. Here political reason mentioned in the sense of exploitation, are detailed in Rosen, J. Stephen and Kurth, James, R., "Testing Theories of Economic Imperialism", Lexington Books, Lexington, 1974.
27. UNCTAD report on "Major issues Arising from he Transfer of Technology to Developing Countries", UNCTAD/TD/B/AC, 11/10 Rev.2.

28. UNCTAD Report on "Restrictive Business Practices in Relation to the Trade and Development of Developing Countries", Report by the Ad-hoc Group of Experts, TD/B-B2/119/REV-1, UNO, New York, 1974.
29. UNCTAD Report on Restrictive Business Practices, TD/B/C-2/Rev.1, New York, 1971.
30. UNCTAD Report on "Restrictive Business Practices in Relation to the Trade, Development of Developing countries", by the Adhoc Group of experts, TD/B-B2/119/Rev.1, UNO, New York, 1974, op. cit.
31. I.L.O. Report on Multinational Enterprise and Social Policy, I.L.O., 1973.
32. UN Report on "The Impact on Multinational Corporations on Development and on International Relations" by Group of 20 eminent persons, New York, May 1974.
33. Kujawa, Duane, "International Labour Relations, Management in Automotive industry: A Comparative study of Chrysler, Ford and General Motors", Peager, Special Studies in International Economics and Development, Peager, New York, 1971.
34. Behrman, Jack N., "National Interest and Multinational Enterprise: Tension among the North Atlantic Countries", Prentice Hall Inc., Engle Wood Cliffs, New Jersey, 1970.
35. Siddharthan, N.S., "Conglomerates and Multinational in India".

3

Intra-Company Transfer Pricing

The contemporary business organisation is a large and complex operation covering many products and services. Management of such an integrated organisation finds it necessary to divide it into certain sub-units or segments each headed by a separate executive. The move towards decentralisation is well pronounced and so is the phenomenon of mergers and acquisitions, that today many companies are structured on some variation of vertical integration. This has rendered the transference of goods and services from one segment to another segment essential. Often the output of one division is the raw material of another division, and so on, until the final product of the company is sold to outside customers. In fact, the use of intra-company transfer pricing gives meaning to the concepts of profit centers and investment centers. Without these prices, many of the responsibility centers would remain only cost centers. A survey of 291 companies conducted by Richard Vancil revealed that 85 per cent of them transferred goods among profit centers and the average value of such transfers accounted for 13 per cent of total cost of the goods sold.

Little wonder that this subject of intra-company transfer pricing, arising out of customer-supplier relationship within the affiliates, has assumed importance in the discipline of cost accounting too. How should the intra-division and intra-product group transfer pricing should be established, so that it provides the needed motivation to the divisional manager and also preserves his autonomy, is a challenging task? That is, when transactions take place between divisions, *inter se*, what is the amount that should be the attached value so as to ensure that the division's interests are made congruent and brought in line with total company interests. This amount is called the transfer price, the charge back or internal price. The discussion is adequate to explain that the transfer pricing, no doubt a question of resource allocation, is often the most troublesome aspect of a control system and has been responsible for a far bit of academic and organisational debate. A conflict of interests can crop up in that a divisional manager acting to maximize the profits of his segment and his own personal compensation may not necessarily be acting to maximize the profits of the group as a whole. The fact is that transfer of goods and services is one of the primary obstacles to meaningful division performance measurement.

Considerations

The decentralisation of firms and the establishment of profit centers have created the need for an internal price system to assist in resource allocation and to motivate managers. Such a system should influence the individual units to promote the welfare of the corporate group as a whole. Transfer pricing is needed to establish congruence between units. Pricing transfers is really a multi dimensional problem and several factors affect the basis of assigning costs to the division acquiring goods and services. In selecting the transfer price, the primary objective should be to pick the one, which assists the management in arriving at the right decision in order to maximize revenues and minimize costs and expenses by divisional segments, and for the full company. Within the overall objective, the prices have to be cost effective and reasonable in the eyes of the affected partners. Then considerations of the nature of business, motivation, degree of control of the market, impact of taxes, etc. have to be given due considerations. A transfer pricing system, which matters good business sense, will usually have the following primary objectives:

- **Apprising Divisional Performance**

A transfer pricing system has to primarily assist top management in appraising and guiding the divisional performance. When information about revenues and expenses is available for individual responsibility centers, it is possible to evaluate the relative performance of each division as well its total contribution to the firm over a span of time. Transfer pricing represents cost to the buyer and revenue to the seller and segmental sales and purchases that affect their performance. Intra-firm transfers inform top management what is really going on. While this may seem very basic, in some cases it appears that top management is not fully informed about sales and profit contribution and the role that transfer pricing plays in determining those contributions.

- **Day Guidance**

Then, transfer pricing provides guidance for the manager whose performance is being evaluated regularly. The manager will be aware of the performance evaluation criteria and able to take action as the facts and circumstances warrant.

- **Autonomy in Decision Making**

Many of the benefits to be derived from decentralisation are based upon the premises that the prerogative of manager, to take decisions for a greater incentive providing the basis for improved performance. The transfer pricing system should allow such autonomy to the managers, what is sometimes referred to as the right of self-governance.

- **Satisfying Tax Authorities**

A transfer pricing system must comply with the various taxation requirements. In an effective system, there should be ample awareness of the legal implications of anti-trust, dumping and custom duties are levied on import prices, but may be adjusted upward if the authorities rule that the transfer prices are not a fair representative of value.

- **Motivation**

Transfer price can be a device to motivate managers to act in the best interest of the company and thereby minimize total company profits. The method should be developed in a manner that it motivates individual managers to reach a decision about selling to or purchasing from other division. Inter-division transfer should be profitable .for the company as a whole as also to be buying and selling units. If an item could be bought cheaply from outside, the system should permit such an arrangement.

Approaches to Transfer Pricing

The literature available on transfer pricing is varied as regards its content and complexity, Abdel Khalik and others have referred to a threefold approach to an intra-company transfer pricing mechanism [1], comprising economic analysis, mathematical programming, and conventional accounting measurements.

Economic Analysis

The tools of micro-economic analysis were first applied to the problem of inter-divisional transfer pricing by Hirshleifer in 1956 [2]. He assumes a firm with two autonomous profit centers, a manufacturing division (selling division) and a distribution division (buying division), each striving to maximize its own profits, possibly subject to restraints or rules imposed by the overall management. Looking at the problem from the point of view of management control, he concludes that in a competitive market marginal cost pricing would produce goal congruent results through autonomous decision making by the two divisions. The situation becomes more complex where imperfect markets are present for the transferred product and this is likely to be more generally the cost. Even in such a case, however, goal congruence can be attained by marginal cost pricing.

Operational Difficulties in Marginal Cost Pricing

The economic analysis model may have conceptual appeal but in practice a number of operational difficulties arise in the course of its implementation. Some significant problems are:

- **Feasibility of Computations**

For marginal cost pricing to be feasible, it is necessary to compute marginal revenue and cost curves. In most situations only the crudest estimates of these marginal quantities are available. The cost data available provide information with regard to variable costs or full costs and not marginal cots. Even if the cumbersome exercise is undertaken to plot marginal curves, these are likely to change rapidly. It would thus involve an enormous amount of work in a multi-division, multi-product firm and in the case of multinationals the problem would be still magnified.

- **Capacity Constraints**

  Capacity constraints may not permit a division to enhance its production to the level where marginal revenue is equal to marginal costs. Consequently, a division would not be anxious to transfer its products to an internal division when it could earn a much higher return in the outside market. If it were compelled to transfer internally, the autonomy of the divisional manager would be violated.

- **Inequities**

  Marginal cost pricing may produce unfair results. The relative profitability of the various units would be determined capriciously, the contribution margin being distributed arbitrarily between the two divisions.

- **Autonomy of Units**

  In imperfectly competitive intermediate markets, achievement of goal congruence requires the headquarter management to play a major role in determining the transfer prices. This amounts to violation of divisional autonomy.

- **Incentive to Overstate Marginal Cost**

  Marginal cost transfer prices also provide an incentive for the managers of the selling division to misrepresent the cost function of producing the supplied product. Thus, by overstating the marginal cost of production the manager will be able to improve the reported performance of the division by obtaining higher transfer prices.

Mathematical Programming

Mathematical programming has been advocated by many as a potential solution to some of the problems encountered when applying the economic model of transfer pricing. Mathematical programming pricing models have been constructed drawing upon linear programming, the decomposition principle and quadratic programming.

The linear programming formulation of transfer pricing problems removes the first two operational difficulties associated with economic models. It does so by introducing linear costs and price assumptions. These assumptions, however, are a close approximation of reality and can be tolerated. Again, linear programming formulation can deal with multiproduct transfers that are exceedingly cumbersome under marginal cost pricing. The other two problems, however, remain. There are gross inequities in the system, as a division with excess capacity has zero dual variables, which means that its transfers to other divisions are at variable costs, whereas transfers from divisions that operate at full capacity may be at more than full costs. Thus, transfer prices determined by linear programming are likely to discourage decisions relating to capacity expansion because such decisions would produce excess capacity, at least in the sort run.

A more serious problem associated with transfer pricing, according to linear programming, is loss in divisional autonomy. Efforts have been made to involve the division in determination of output levels. For instance, the decomposition model proposed by Maumol and Fabian recommended an iterative process for setting transfer prices, which is as follows:

1. Based upon known cost and capacity constraints of the various divisions, headquarters propose a set of transfer prices for the various divisions by employing a mathematical programming procedure.
2. Based on these internal transfer prices, the divisions determine their optimal results and report them back to headquarters, together with their resultant demands.
3. The headquarters then use these results to calculate new transfer prices based on the new set of interdivisional demands. The division then proceeds to calculate new requirements based upon the revised transfer price.

This iterative process is repeated until the transfer prices reported back to the division do not change. [3]

This procedure is a form of disguised centralisation. Though it does restore a measure of divisional autonomy, transfer prices are determined centrally and headquarters also determines the divisional output. Besides, as the information needs are not known with certainty, it diminishes the generally viability of the model. Again, the behavioral problems anticipated under the model are self-defeating.

Conventional Accounting Measures of Cost

The third approach is based on the conventional accounting measures of cost. It draws upon easily accessible internal cost data and uses these figures in various modified forms to determine the prices. This is the most pragmatic approach and is discussed in the following sections. Under this approach, the transfer pricing methods used in actual practice can be classified into three main categories, namely cost-based, market-based and others. Variations exist, within each category and occasionally, a hybrid form is also used, i.e. a combination of cost-based and other methods (see Figure 3.1).

- **Cost Based Systems**

Cost based transfer prices are a popular pricing mechanism in circumstances where market prices are not feasible either because they are not available or are otherwise unsuitable. In most cases of vertical transfer, to successive levels of production or distribution, where the transferring unit is viewed as a cost center, the cost-based methods of transfer pricing are applied.

Analogously, horizontal transfer, to similar levels of production or distribution by captive units is also usually executed at cost, which may include freight and handling charges. The more centralised firms tend to favour cost-based transfers as a basis for control, decision-making and monitoring performance. Cost-based transfer transfers may take various forms; they may be at (a) full cost (b) modified cost, (c) standard cost, and (d) partial cost.

(a) Full Cost

Perhaps the least satisfactory transfer price is a mechanical full cost pricing system. Under this method, the price is determined by including all direct and indirect costs, fixed as well

Figure 3.1: Transfer Pricing Alternatives under Conventional Cost Approach

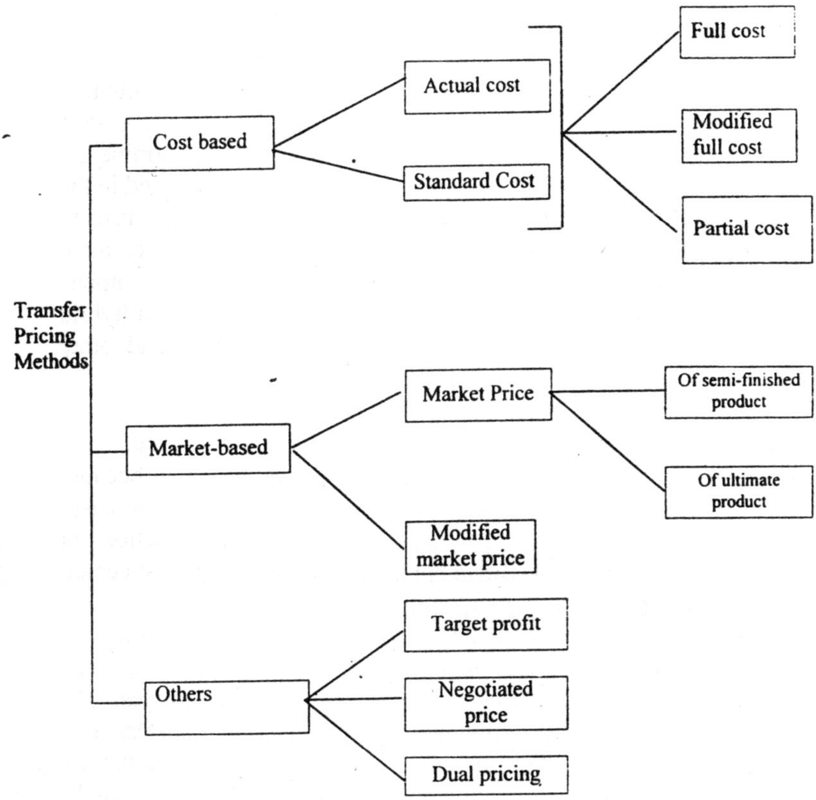

as variable. The advantages frequently cited of a historic cost transfer price are that it is simple, definitely determinable and readily available. Besides, it is easy to defend externally to the government and other regulatory agencies. Again, it is argued that fixed costs usually form an ingredient of long-run decisions, hence ought to be included in the transfer prices.

The method, however, suffers from numerous shortcomings. Transfers at actual costs fail to provide the supplying division with incentive to control its costs. A blank permit to transfer at actual costs may, therefore, eliminate the stimulus for production efficiently and cost reduction. Consequently, the inefficiencies of the selling division are passed on to the buying segment of the firm, which adversely affects its competitive position in the external market. Nor is it an appropriate guide for evaluating the divisional performance. Profits cannot be used as motivators for the transferring division. Cost being the basis for intermediate transfer, profits will be recorded by he final transferees only. Such transfer prices are also not very helpful to the transferees in the process of decision-making, unless variable costs are reflected separately. Consequently, at times, decision, that is dysfunctional for the firm as a whole may be taken.

Suppose M and N are two divisions of a company P. M supplies certain components to N at full cost of Rs.250 per unit (this includes Rs.100 fixed overhead costs). N incurs an additional cost of Rs.70 per unit to process and market the final product. Both the units are operating at less than full capacity. An external supplier Q offers to sell the component to N for Rs.200 per unit. Assuming further than N can sell the product for a maximum price of Rs. 350, it would find it profitable to purchase the component from Q rather than from M as it would improve its performance by Rs.50 per unit. The question is – would this decision taken by N be optimal for the company as a whole? An analysis of the situation is presented in Table 3.1.

The table reveals that the firm as a whole would benefit to the extent of Rs.50 per unit if N purchases the component from M instead of Q. As the transfer prices are based on full costs N is led to treat Ms fixed cost as variable rendering the decision to purchase from Q dysfunctional for the firm as a whole

Table-3.1
Impact of N's Decision on the Firm as a Whole

(Rs.)	When purchased from M (Internally)	When purchased from Q (externally)
Additional revenue/unit	Rs.350	Rs.350
Additional cost/unit		
M Rs.150*		
Q		
N Rs.70	Rs.220	
	Rs. 70	Rs.270
Benefit as a whole	Rs.130	Rs. 80

* Only variable costs of M would be relevant here.

(b) Modified Cost

In practice, many variations of the cost based methods have been developed. A common variant is the full cost plus transfer pricing method. Under this model, the cost of the product or service is inflated by some amount. The addition may take the form of a fixed amount per unit or it may be a percentage of the cost. The method attempts to overcome some of the shortcomings of the full cost method. It would provide the benefit of profit as a motivator. Besides, in situations where pricing practices must be defended, cost plus method often satisfies the arm's length criteria. However, it is doubtful whether cost-plus transfer prices (where actual costs are used for computation) would provide any incentive for efficiency on the part of the selling division. On the contrary, the selling division would generate more profits by incurring more costs. For instance, assume that the method provides for a ten per cent plus on actual costs and cost of production of the selling division is Rs.100 per unit. A profit of

Rs.10 per unit is generated for the division. On the other hand, if the costs increase to Rs.120 the division would be generating a profit of Rs.12 per unit of the product transferred. This problem of the selling division profiting from its own inefficiencies is eliminated when standard costs are used as the base for cost plus transfers. Also, the modified cost model fails to serve the purpose of decision-making.

(c) Standard Cost

Substitution of standard or budgeted costs for actual costs could rectify the shortcoming of the earlier method where inefficiencies are passed on to the buying unit in the form of inflated prices. Under this method, price to the buying division is based on efficient performance. Inefficient operations are detected early, hence, they are not carried through to the final product. Standard costs provide the incentive to operate efficiently as the transferring unit is not permitted to recover costs of its inefficiencies from the buying division. Standard costs, however, would not avoid the more serious problem of sub-optimal decision-making.

(d) Partial Cost

A modified version of the full cost approach is the method under which only part of the costs are considered for setting the transfer price. The partial costs generally taken into account are the variable costs of manufacturing the product. This method is advantageous in so far as control of relevant costs is concerned. By aiding in the cost and input decisions, it minimizes the possibilities of purchase from outsiders at higher costs to the organization.

Criticism generally levied against the variable cost method is that is further removed from sensibility to market factors. Lack of consideration for fixed expenses and capital employed is likely to influence long term profitability. Again, this method being based only on costs, profits have no role in motivating and evaluating the performance of the divisions. Yet more weighty criticism is the one advanced in case of international transactions: use of this method of pricing would lead to charge of dumping being levied against the transferor as these prices would not be representative of economic substance nor fulfil the arm's length criterion.

At times an additive is applied to the variable costs to motivate the divisional managers. This only serves to blunt the utility of the transfer price so determined as decision tools and is therefore rarely used in actual practice.

Market Price Based Systems

Transfer prices based on market price may be based on the market price of the semi-finished product, or on the ultimate market price.

(a) Based on Semi-Finished Product

There is a general agreement that if competitive markets for the intermediate product exist, market prices would be the ideal transfer price; the reason being that it is determined by parties that are external to the firm and deal at arm's length with one another. Market price, when used for internal transfers is, therefore, the most objective measure of value employed while charging for the goods or services exchanged. As Horngren puts it:

"When an organisation has profit centers, market prices should be the prime candidate for setting transfer prices. In this way buyers and sellers systematically keep abreast of their internal and external opportunities, and problems of congruence, effort and autonomy are minimized". [4]

Market oriented transfer prices offer numerous benefits to the concerns employing them. Use of market price is consistent with decentralised profit centers orientation. Profits determined by external markets are less subject to internal manipulations and are a reasonable measure of performance. Shillinglaw and Burton have expressed the objectivity of transfer pricing at market price as follows:

"A transfer price system based on market price has considerable appeal. It seems a fair, objective measure of the value of the product transferred. It introduces external competitiveness pressure, and standards, and it measures divisional profits in terms of external opportunities". [5]

Market based transfer price help to distinguish between profitable and non-profitable operations. Competitive market prices thus stimulate control of costs and encourage efficiency. Market prices easily fit into the notion of arm's length price. Among host governments sensitive to anti-competitive practices, a consensus seems to be emerging that arm's length pricing is an appropriate nom in computing taxable profits.

The benefits, which accrue from market based transfer prices, should not lead one to the conclusion that they are free from shortcomings. Market price is the appropriate transfer only where the commodity being transferred is produced in a competitive market, that is, competitive in the theoretical sense, where no single producer considers himself large enough to influence price by his own output decision. A major problem associated with market price is the frequent absence of an intermediate market for the product or service in question. This happens in the case of semi-finished products or specialized components. For instance, where the product or service is specially made for a particular division, or has special characteristics, market price would only give a rough estimate of the market value of the specific product or service. Besides, decisions regarding internal transfer made on the basis of market price, under normal operating conditions, at less than full capacity, may not be congruent with the best interests of the total enterprise. The management is not left with much scope to adjust prices for competitive and strategic purposes under this mechanism of transfer pricing. Again, overemphasis on market prices may result in the lack of adequate attention to control of costs.

(b) Based on Ultimate Market Price

This category includes the sales minus method. Under this method, the basis of transfer pricing is found in the price realized by the marketing division, which sells the product to third parties. The transfer price is determined by reducing this price by an amount (usually a percentage) considered appropriate to cover the expenses of the marketing division in acting as an independent distributor. This method of transfer pricing would be appropriate in cases where the marketing division has no production of its own but is merely involved in selling and distribution activities. Determination of the level of allowance for profit is a difficulty generally encountered under this mechanism. One alternative is to permit an allowance in consonance with comparable enterprises in the same industry. Another possibility is to deduct a percentage of cost or turnover which would be enough to cover selling and distribution expenses and also the profit mark-up.

A leading automobile manufacturing company in India follows the policy of transfer price as a proportion of selling price. The tractor, motorcycle and spares manufacturing divisions transfer the final product to the marketing division at 97.5 per cent of the selling price. The profit of the market division is found after deducting its expenses (selling, administrative and allocation of head office expenses) from 2.5 per cent of the selling price.

Modified Market Price

Market price is sometimes modified to reflect the specific situation involved 'n the intra-company transfers of products and services. The market price may be reduced to make allowance for reduced effort in selling and transportation expenses that often characterize inter-divisional transfer. The justification put forward is that since the selling division would be incurring less cost in making a sale to another division, part of the savings should be passed on to the buying division.

This method would, however, not be very appropriate where transfers are made among subsidiaries situated in two different countries owing to the distance involved, economies on shipping, etc., would not be realized. In certain situations, however, it may be necessary to revise the market price upwards to take care of hidden costs arising on account of the buying division making reasonable delivery demands on the selling division or the extra cost incurred to meet a more stringent quality standard.

Others

This category may include transfers on the basis of (a) negotiated price, (b) target profit, and (c) dual price.

(a) Negotiated Price

This mechanism represents a refinement of the market based transfer prices. It is also termed as bargained price. As its name indicates, this price is determined by bargaining between the subunits involved. It suggests an arm's length bargaining process such as would be encountered when dealing with entities external to the firm. The negotiation approach rests on the assumption that the entities have complete freedom to bargain. In other words, if an agreement were not reached on the transfer price they would be free to sell in the external market. In the absence of availability of such alternatives, the negotiation approach would break down. Kaplan and Atkinson refer to certain conditions that are essential for the negotiated price technique to succeed. These include:

1. Some form of outside market for the intermediate product. This avoids a bilateral monopoly situation in which the final price could vary over too wide a range, depending on the strength and skill of negotiators.
2. Sharing of all market information among the negotiators. This should enable the negotiated price to be close to the opportunity cost of one, or preferably both, the divisions.
3. Freedom to buy or sell outside. This provides the necessary discipline to the bargaining process.
4. Support and occasional involvement of top management. But such involvement must be done with restraint and tact, if it is not to undermine the negotiating process. [6]

There are certain advantages attached to the negotiated price approach. Bargaining makes adjustments for unusual or inappropriate aspects of the market price. Where both parties are open to reasonable concessions, negotiations would improve the use of economic resources in situations where excess capacity exists.

The negotiated price mechanism, however, is not free from defects. The negotiation process no doubt consumes useful management time of both the parties involved and also the top management, which is required to oversee the negotiating process and to mediate disputes. The measurement of divisional profitability is rendered sensitive to the negotiating skills of the managers. Besides, captive units are generally placed at a relative disadvantage in such negotiation. In situations where the negotiated price is above the opportunity cost of supplying the transferred goods, it may lead to sub optimal levels of output. Despite its limitations, however, the negotiated price mechanism seems to be the most practical method for establishing the transfer price between two divisions.

(b) Target Profit Price

The approaches discussed so far are either cost oriented or market based, another approach suggested by Heitger and Matulich is to arrive at a transfer price based on a target profit. According to them, "Target profit transfer prices attempt to provide reasonable or desired profit levels for divisions when a market price is not available or when other transfer pricing methods would yield unsatisfactory results". [7] Thus, under this method the transfer price is designed to provide a reasonable profit to the selling division, say 10 per cent of the standard costs or actual costs. To illustrate, assume that Sunset Limited has two divisions – a manufacturing division and an assembly division. The units produced by manufacturing division are transferred to the assembly division and the policy of the company is to provide a divisional profit of 30 per cent on sales with standard costs as the base. The cost data of the manufacturing division is presented in Table 3.2.

To determine the transfer price it is essential to first compute the total revenue required to yield the target profit. This figure would then be divided by the units produced to obtain the transfer price. The computation therefore is:

$$TR = 0.3\ TR + TSC$$

$$TR = 0.3\ TR + (1,60,000 + 50,000)$$

0.7TR=2,10,000
TR= 2,10,000 divided by 0.7
= 3,00,000

Table 3.2

	Standard Costs (in Rs.)	**Actual costs (in Rs.)**
Standard units	20,000	
Units produced		20,000
Manufacturing expenses	1, 60,000	1,97,600
Operating expenses	50,000	82,400
Total costs	2,10,000	2,80,000

Where TR represents total revenue and TSC represents total standard costs.

Thus, Rs.3,00,000 is the total revenue required to generate a 30 per cent profit on sales using standard costs as the base. The transfer price per unit is therefore equal to Rs.3,00,000 divided by 20,000 i.e. Rs.15 per unit.

Had the profits been measured against actual cost, the process of computation would have been similar except that actual cost would have been substituted for standard cost. Thus:

TR= 0.3TR + TAC
TR= 0.3 TR + 1,97,600 + 82,400
0.7 TR=2,80,000
= 2,80,000 divided by 0.7
TR= 4,00,000

Where TAC represents total actual costs.

The transfer price would be fixed at Rs.4,00,000 divided by 20,000=Rs.20 per unit.

The situation becomes slightly more complicated when the transferring division sells part of its product to the outside market. In such cases, to determine the transfer price, the revenue obtained from outside sales would be deducted from the desired total revenue and the difference divided by the number of units transferred internally. In the previous example, assume that the manufacturing division sells 15 per cent of its output to an outside buyer @ Rs.20 per unit. The targeted profit continues to be 30 per cent of sales using standard costs. The transfer price will be computed as follows:

The total revenue required will be the same as the target profit and the standard costs are the same. Thus:

TR= 0.3 TR + (1,60,000 + 50,000)

TR= Rs.3,00,000

Revenue generated from outside sales = 3,000 x Rs.20 = Rs.60,000

Revenue to be generated from internal sales = 3,00,000-60,000 = Rs.2,40,000

Transfer price= Rs.2,40,0000 divided by 17,000=Rs.14.12 approx.

(c) Dual Pricing

Since it is virtually impossible for a single transfer price to simultaneously meet the criteria of goal congruence, sub unit autonomy and managerial effort, some companies resort to dual pricing. Under this mechanism a given transaction is recorded at two prices arrived at by using two different methods. This system has gained acceptance over the years as it attempts to reconcile the objectives of control, performance evaluation and decision-making. Most of the complex enterprises operate somewhere along the centralised-decentralised continuum. The cost center approach would be most appropriate in case of some units; a profit center approach would be more suited for others. To illustrate, where a company has a captive central manufacturing unit and a distribution unit, the manufacturing unit may be controlled internally by using a standard cost plus mechanism of transfer pricing for transfers to the distribution unit. The transferee unit, however, would be charged only the standard cost. This will enhance decision making at that level and at subsequent levels. The method, however, suffers from the drawback that it would result in some double counting of profits and so the aggregate of divisional profits would not reflect the profits of the enterprise as a whole. Another argument put forward against its use is that it would lead to deterioration in control of costs at all levels. This situation, however, would not necessarily result in all cases, as it would depend on the caliber and astuteness of the management.

The pros and cons of the different transfer pricing models discussed so far give us an insight into their nature but do not provide an answer as to which model is optimal. There is seldom a single transfer price model that can ensure the desired results. As Merville and Petty observe,

"The transfer pricing issue has been addressed from a variety of perspectives and vantage points, however, endeavors to construct an all purpose intra-company price have produced more questions than answers". [8]

The argument is that an appropriate transfer price is dependent upon numerous factors such as economic and legal circumstances and the decision at hand. One transfer pricing model may be required for motivation and another for evaluation. Again, what may be an optimal price for tax purposes may not be so for other external purposes. Concisely stated, the appropriate determination of a transfer price must be aligned with the end objective. As Sharav puts it,

"What, if any, is the 'preferred method' of transfer pricing? No method that has emerged to date, be it cost, - or market based, has been immune from criticism. The practices of actual companies involved in transfer pricing demonstrate a consistent rejection of any dogmatic and singular approach, no matter how theoretically superior it may have been proclaimed. Users and uses determine the transfer pricing technique to be selected". [9]

Though there is no all-pervasive rule for transfer pricing which would lead to optimal decisions for an organisation as a whole. Horngren and Foster have devised a general rule, which according to them, has proved to be helpful in setting a transfer price. Accordingly, Minimum Transfer Price=Additional outlay costs incurred per unit to point of transfer +Opportunity costs per unit to the firm as a whole.

The outlay costs is defined as the cash outflows that are directly associated with the production and transfer of the products and services. Opportunity costs on the other hand, represent the maximum contribution foregone by the company when the product or service is transferred internally. This distinction between outlay and opportunity costs is necessitated by the fact that the accounting system typically records only outlay costs. Where a perfectly competitive intermediate market exists, the opportunity cost will be the market price minus the outlay costs. For instance, if the outlay cost of a product is Rs.25 per unit and the market price is Rs.40 per unit, assuming that a perfectly competitive intermediate market exists, the transfer price will be Rs.40 per unit arrived at as follows:

$$\begin{aligned} TP &= OtC + OpC \\ &= 25 + (MP - OtC) \\ &= 25 + (40 - 25) \\ &= 25 + 15 \\ &= Rs.40 \end{aligned}$$

where TP denotes transfer price, OtC outlay costs, OpC, opportunity costs and MP the market price.

Transfer Pricing of Services

Numerous methods have been devised successfully for transfer pricing of products exchanged within the company. However, in the increasingly services oriented business world, most companies encounter significant hurdles in devising an appropriate transfer pricing mechanism for services. The challenges arise on accounts of the peculiar feature of services as compared to commodities. In the first instance, as services are intangible it is difficult to define exactly what is for sale, that is the product content. This feature creates a problem for sellers to defend or buyers to understand the prices of services. Besides, the skill and experience of the personnel involves challenges of proper evaluation. To understand how companies formulate transfer pricing policies for services a survey was conducted by Keegan and Howard of Price Waterhouse. [10] According to their findings, historically services have been transferred at cost or at a mandated market price, equivalent to standard cost plus a mark-up.

In recent years, however, with burgeoning white-collar workforce many large companies expect market-based transfer pricing to play a more important role in structuring relationships between internal service organisations and core operations. The survey reveals that establishing an external market price is always troublesome in a transfer pricing system. It is relatively easy to identify market-based prices for commodity like services, such as order of catalogue items. This mechanism would, however, be inappropriate for customary services like executive recruitment, etc. In situations like 82 per cent of the companies' surveyed report that transfer prices of similar services provided by outside vendors frequently serve as the basis for this negotiation. They suggest that in order to reduce the potential for disputes among internal buyers and sellers, the corporate financial staff must issue definitive guidelines for transfer pricing services based on factors such as substitutability, volume and costs. The objectives of transfer pricing exercise a decisive influence on the method to be adopted. The objectives of transfer pricing are discussed in the following section.

Transfer Pricing in Multinational Firms

The issues involved in fixing of transfer prices in the case of a multinational firm are slightly different than that of a multi-division company operating within a country. For the multinational firms, transfer pricing must accomplish two objectives, such as performance evaluation and optimum determination of income taxes.

- **Performance Evaluation**

Subsidiaries are frequently evaluated on the basis of net income and return on investment. [11] As is the case for any transfer price, the selling subsidiary wants a high transfer price that will raise its net income. The buying subsidiary wants a low transfer price that will provide better margins and increase its net income. Transfer prices in MNCs are frequently set by the parent company. Therefore, the use of mandated transfer prices makes the use of ROI and net income suspect. That is, they are not under the control of division managers and no longer serve as an indicator of management performance.

- **Income Tax and Transfer Pricing**

If all the countries have the same tax structure, then transfer prices would be set independently of taxes. However, reality is different. There are high tax countries (like the United States) and low tax countries (such as Cayman Island). As a result, MNCs may use transfer pricing to shift cost to high tax countries and shift revenues to low tax countries. Table 3.3 illustrates this concept, as two transfer prices are set. The first transfer price is \$100 as title for the goods passes from the Belgian Subsidiary to the re-invoicing center. Since the first transfer price is equal to full cost, profit is zero and taxes on zero profit are also nil. The second transfer price is set at \$200 by the re-invoicing center in Puerto Rico. The transfer from Puerto Rico to the United States does result in profit, but this profit does not result in any tax liability because Puerto Rico has no corporate income tax. Finally, the US subsidiary sells the product to the external party at the \$200 transfer price. Again, price equals cost, so there is no profit on which to pay income taxes. Without the re-invoicing center, the goods would have gone directly from Belgium to the United States. If the transfer price were set at \$200, the profit in Belgium would have been \$100 subject to the 42 per cent tax rate. Alternatively, if the transfer price set was \$100, no Belgian tax would have been paid, but the US subsidiary would have realized a profit of \$1000 and that would have been subject to the US corporate Income Tax rate of 35 per cent. US based multinationals are subject to Internal Revenue Service (IRS) code section 482 on the pricing of inter company transactions. This section gives the IRS the authority to reallocate income and deductions among subsidiaries if it believes that such reallocation will reduce potential tax evasion.

Table 3.3: Use of Transfer Pricing to Affect Taxes Paid

Action	Tax Impact
Belgian subsidiary to parent company produces a component at a cost of $100 per unit title to the component is transferred to a Re-invoicing center in Puerto Rico at a transfer Price of $100 per unit.	42% tax rate $100 revenue - $100 cost = $0 Tax paid= $ 0
RE-invoicing Center in Puerto Rico, also a subsidiary of parent company, transfers title of component to US Subsidiary of parent company at a transfer price of $200 per unit.	0% tax rate $200 revenue - $100 cost = $100 Tax paid = $ 0
US subsidiary sells component to external company at $200 each	35% tax rate $200 Revenue - $200 Cost = $0, taxes paid=$ 0

Basically, Section 482 requires that sales be made at "arm's length". That is, the transfer price set should match the price that would be set if the transfer were being made by unrelated parties. The IRS allows three pricing methods that approximate arm's length pricing. In order of preference these are the comparable uncontrolled price method, the resale price method, and the cost plus method. The comparable uncontrolled price method is essentially market price. The resale price method is equal to the sale price received by the reseller less an appropriate mark-up – that is, the subsidiary purchasing a product for resale sets a transfer price equal to the resale price less gross profit. Percentage of the cost-plus method is simply the cost based transfer price.

Of course, MNCs also subject to taxation by other countries as well as the United States. Since income taxes are virtually universal, consideration of income tax effects prevails in management decision-making. Manager may legally avoid taxes, they may not evade them. MNCs may have tax – planning information systems that attempt to accomplish global tax minimization.

Survey of Company Practices

Table 3.4 summarizes the factors that executives consider important when determining transfer prices for both domestic and multinational operations. Table 3.5 summarizes the result of studies of domestic transfer pricing method. Observe the widespread use of both market based and full cost based transfer prices. For companies using cost based methods, standard costs are more widely used than actual costs. One survey of US companies reports that standard costs were used by 54% of respondents, actual cost method was used by 16% of the companies surveyed and some of each method was used by 30% of the respondents. [12] Organisations differ in how they handle transfer pricing disputes. Approaches used in practice include the following. [13]

Table 3.4: Factors that Executives Consider Important on Transfer Pricing (in Order of Importance)

A. DOMESTIC TRANSFER PRICING [14]

1. Performance evaluation – to measure the result of each operating sub unit
2. Managerial motivation – to provide the company with a "profit-making" orientation throughout each organisational sub unit.

3. Pricing and product emphasis – to better reflect "Costs" and "Margins" that must be received from customers
4. External market recognition – to maintain an internal competitiveness so that the company stay in balance with outside market forces

B MULTINATIONAL TRANSFER PRICING [15]

1. Overall income to the company
2. The competitive position of subsidiaries in foreign countries
3. Performance evaluation of foreign subsidiaries
4. Restrictions imposed by foreign countries on repatriation of income or dividend
5. The need to maintain adequate cash flows in foreign subsidiaries.
6. Maintaining good relationship with host government

Conclusion

For intracompany transfer pricing, although a number of methods have been developed for the years, there is no final answer to the problem: There is no, and there cannot be "one correct approach" to the issue. Policies tend to vary for different types of products and services within the same organisation of all, the trading price based upon external market conditions appears to be most satisfactory method as it would considerably reduce the extent of possible manipulation and satisfy the test of objectivity. Where such external prices are not available for intermediate products especially when they are of a specialized character, negotiated prices should be adopted. But, these should be reviewed every six months or every year. The dual or two-step pricing could also be tried to mitigate the difficulties associated with the problem. However, despite extensive literature on the subject, "optimum" transfer pricing method for management purposes remains a goal rather than a reality. The unresolved

Table 3.5: Surveys of Transfer Pricing Method

A. Domestic Transfer Pricing Methods

Methods	United States*	Australia**	Canada***	Japan*	India****	U.K.
1. Market Price based	30%	13%	34%	34%	47%	41%
2. Cost Based: Variable Cost	4	N.D.	6	2	6	6
Absorption or full cost	45	N.D.	37	44	47	19
Others	1	N.D.	3	-	-	4
Total 3. Negotiated 4. Other	50% 18% 2%	65% 11% 11%	46% 18% 2%	46% 19% 1%	53% - -	29% 24% 6%
	100%	100%	100%	100%	100%	100%

Contd...

B. Multinational Transfer –Pricing Methods

Methods	United States*	Australia**	Canada***	Japan*	India****	U.K.
1. Market Price based	35%	-	37%	37%	-	31%
2. Cost Based: Variable Cost	2	-	5	3	-	5
Absorption or full cost	42	-	26	38	-	28
Others	2	-	2	-	-	5
Total	46%	-	33%	41%	-	38%
3. Negotiated	14%	-	26%	22%	-	20%
4. Others	5%	-	4%	-	-	11%
	100%	-	100%	100%	-	100%

Sources:

* R.Tang, C Walter and R.Raymond "Transfer Pricing – Japanese V/s American Style, "Management Accounting January, 1979 pp.12 – 16.

** P.Blayney and M.Joye, "Cost Accounting Practices in Australian Manufacturing Companies", Working Paper, University of Sydney, 1989.

*** R.Tang "Canadian Transfer pricing practices", in C.A.Magazine March, 1980, pp 32-38

****V.Govindarajan and B.Ramamurthy, " Transfer Pricing Policies in Indian Companies: A Survey", Chartered Accountant, Nov.1983 pp.296 – 301.

- N.D. means not disclosed.

problem is one of developing a set of transfer prices that will simultaneously guide a division's decisions in the best long-run interests of the firm and also serve as an equitable price for measuring divisional performance.

At the same time, the study by Vancil quoted earlier, reveals that the negotiations, is by far the most popular method (22% of the divisionalised manufacturing companies applying it), followed by listed market price (17.2%), full actual cost (13%), full standard cost (12.5%), competitor's price (11.7%), and full cost plus mark-up (10.9%).

Notes

1. Rashad A. Khalik, A. and Lusk E.J., "Transfer pricing – A Synthesis. The Accounting Review", Vol.49, pp 8-23, January, 1974
2. Hirshleifer J., "On the Economics of Transfer Pricing", "The Journal of Business", Vol. 29, pp. 172-184, July 1956.
3. Baumol, W.J., and Fabian, T., "Decomposition, Pricing for Decentralised and External Economies", Management Sciences, Vol.10, pp. 1-31, July 1964.
4. Horngren,C.T., "Introduction of Management Accounting", 6th ed., Prentice-Hall of India, New Delhi, 1984.
5. Shillinglaw, G. and Burton J.C., "Materials Management and Profit-Center Concept", Management Bulletin 4, American Management Association, 1964.
6. Kalpan, R. and Atkinson, A.A., "Advanced Management Accounting", 2nd ed., Prentice Hall, Inc., Englewood Cliffs, New Jersey, 1989.
7. Heitger, L.E. and Matulich, S., "Managerial Accounting", McGraw Hill International, Japan, 1982.
8. Merville, L.J., and Petty W.J., "Transfer Price for the Multination Firm", Accounting Review, Vol. 53, pp. 935-951, October 1978.
9. Sharav, I., "Transfer Pricing – Diversity of Goals and Practices", The Journal of Accountancy. Vol. 138, pp. 55-62, April 1974.
10. Keegan D.P., and Howard, P.D., "Making Transfer Prices Work for Services", Journal of Accountancy, Vol. 165, No. 3, pp. 96-103, March 1988.

11. A study of seventy multinational revealed that 80 per cent used these measures. See Heler Gernon Morsicato, "Currency Translation and Performance Evaluation in Multinationals" (Ann Arbor UMI Research Press, 1982).
12. "Transfer Pricing Practices of American Industry" (New York: Price Waterhouse, 1984).
13. R.Eccles, "Analyzing your Company is Transfer Pricing Practices" Journal of Cost Management, Summer, 1987.
14. Source Price Waterhouse, "Transfer Pricing Practices of American Industry" p.2.
15. Source R. Tang "Environmental Variable of Multinational Transfer Pricing: A UK Perspective", Journal of Business Finance & Accounting, Vol. 9 No. 2 p.182.

4

Transfer Pricing and Performance Evaluation

As corporations have grown in size and are more widespread in operations, they are necessarily divisionalised organizations. An organization becomes large either through internal expansion and diversification, or externally by merger and acquisition. It well suits such an entity to divide its operations into smaller segments, divisions, departments, subsidiaries, and affiliates. Decentralization enhances the efficiency and effectiveness of managing the business. When authority is delegated to the managers of business sub-divisions, their morale and level of job satisfaction get richer because of their active participation in decision-making. They may be more motivated resulting in better decisions and greater efficiency. Made into a miniature of the competitive free enterprise system, an independent division, on the whole, works better. How advantageous is such decentralization has been spelled out by Shillinglaw [1]:

(i) By transferring decision making responsibility of executives they can devote all of their efforts to individual markets or product lines.

(ii) By bringing subordinate executives into more direct control with the ultimate profit executives of the firm, they are motivated towards these objectives.

(iii) By providing an integrated training ground for top managers of the future.

(iv) However, the fact remains that successful firms are those that have achieved a right trade-off between integration and differentiation.

An important function of an accounting in a decentralized organization is reporting the performance of managers. It is a necessary part of corporate control system. The corporate headquarters must secure a quantification of the degree and efficiency with which the objectives assigned to the division have been accomplished from year to year. Managers of a business are accountable to the suppliers of capital for the ways in which the capital has been used to meet the stated objectives.

Performance Measurements

Divisional performance measurement is a multi-dimensional exercise. For appraising current operating performance; both profit and non-profit criteria, have been employed. Let these be explained in detail:

Non-Profit Measurements

It is widely accepted that performance alone fails to report the total functioning of a subsidiary or division. Simply concentrating on profit will give an inadequate picture of what a segment has done to promote its own and corporate goals. Depending upon some measure of profitability to the disregard of other yardsticks such as quality of goods and services, market share or market penetration, employee morale, discovery of new products, etc. is not safe. Managerial performance has many dimensions and multiple measurements to be employed. General Electric Inc., USA, for example, has catalogued of result areas to assess the contribution of a functional unit. These are profitability, market position, productivity, product leadership, personal development, employee attitude towards public responsibility, and balance.

Financial Indicators

Profit is the most significant aspect of performance evaluation. Everything ultimately boils down to the bottom of income statement. Unless revenue exceeds the cost, except the early period, no unit or division is worthy of continuing. It must break-even the sooner it can, and then start generating surpluses for the corporation. Its eventual success is to be judged by a sustained rise in the profit curve. In any management control systems, the analysis of profitability by operating divisions' or product lines is the central component. Some of the non-profit criteria listed above are used as supplements to the principal profitability criterion.

In practice, one finds four financial measurements for rating the performance of decentralized operations. These are:

(i) Net income
(ii) Contribution margin
(iii) Return on investment (ROI)
(iv) Residual income (RI)

Let these be discussed in detail, but this much can be observed at this stage, that the first two measures are now only of the theoretical importance in as much as these give absolute profit amount. The latter two are relative measures, and are considered prime indicators of profitability of a unit. Between ROI and RI, there has been a debate about the relative superiority, but the prevalent practice now is to use them together. However, an accounting method used for the purpose should have some attributes. It should provide an equitable and comparable measure of performance for its managers. Further, while it should promote autonomy, it should assure that the segment does not behave in a manner detrimental to the overall goals of the corporation. The choice of an appropriate accounting system, therefore, becomes vital to the evaluation of decentralized organizations.

Net Income

Net income or net profit is an accounting concept which means revenue less expense. It is the incurred excess of sales revenue earned over expenses incurred. These expenses are all variable and fixed costs, or product and period costs. Net income measures a segment's success in accomplishing its primary objective to increase owner's equity. This is, essentially an external reporting figure and is based on absorption costing system. But it has been used for comparing the current operating performance of segments *inter se*.

Net income as a measure of performance evaluation has obvious limitations. Since it is rooted in full costing system, assigns indirect, joint and common costs to divisions, which is a subjective and arbitrary process. It also charges non-recurring items such as extraordinary gains and losses, interest expense and accelerated provision for depreciation, which are uncontrollable by divisions. Further, absolute figures of net income mean little by themselves unless compared with; say net sales or net investment. These statistics may induce the manager to accept any project so long as here is an excess of revenue overcost. Hence, despite its age and clarity, net income has not been considered a reliable indicator of divisional performance.

Contribution Margin

Contribution margin is also called 'traceable profit'; it is the difference between sale revenue and variable costs. It is the excess of revenues over variable costs associated with a segment. Contribution margin represents the amount available after sales revenue has covered all variable costs. The resulting figure indicates the contribution of each deviation towards the recovery of unallocated fixed costs of the central corporate facilities.

It may be noted that the basic data used for both net income and contribution margin is the same. In the later, costs tend to get classified into variable and fixed components according to their behaviour in response to changes in volume of activity. It is an internal reporting concept, and is based on direct costing system. The merit of contribution margin is this analysis of costs recording to their behavioural pattern into variable and fixed, and controllable and uncontrollable categories. It thus, becomes a more dependable measure of the ability of segments to recover the common costs from their operations, and yet contribute to the corporate pool of profits. At the same time, contribution margin reporting also is an absolute measure with all its limitations. Further, it focuses on short-run profitability, and is most sensitive to management decisions. Notwithstanding, segment contribution margin as a useful devise, it has been extensively employed to gauge the divisional performance.

Segment Contribution Margin

In the case of divisional performance, it is the segment contribution, which is a relevant measure. Here also, variable costs are deducted from the sales revenue. But in addition to variable costs, all direct fixed costs which relate to the segment are sub-treated. The segment margin analysis differentiates between avoidable and unavoidable fixed costs and subtracts the avoidable fixed costs from segment revenue in as much as these are directly attributable to segment operation and would be avoided if the segment is discontinued. The following figures help illustrate the working and significance of segment contribution margin:

Sales	13,00,000
Less variable expenses	6,30,000
Contribution margin	6,70,000
Less direct fixed costs	2,10,000
Segment margin	4,60,000

If indirect fixed costs allocated to be segment for the period have been of Rs.2,40,000/-, the segment net income will be Rs.2,20,000/-.

The utility of this approach can be considered in a situation where the contribution margin is positive, but segment margin is negative. This indicates that while variable costs are being covered, avoidable fixed costs of the segment are not being recouped. The viability of the segment, therefore, is in question, and the decision may be to discontinue the segment, as the corporate income thereby will increase. The discontinuance decision, however, involves so many other variables, including the time frame.

Returns on Investment

Over the years, return on investment has been the widely used measure of divisional performance. In an investment centre, emphasis is on return on investment rather than on profit. The management tires to find out the percentage profit the division is earning on the investment committed therein. The equation is:

$$ROI = \frac{\text{Net income}}{\text{Investment Base}} \times 100$$

The net income annually is operating income i.e. earnings before interest and taxes (EBIT). Since interest and taxes differ in different divisions due to several reasons, EBIT is a fair numerator. The investment base usually is net assets i.e. gross assets employed less accumulated depreciation thereon till date. It is the investment made by all types of proprietors and creditors in return to which profit-ability has to be judged. However, following the large chemical giant of the USA, E.I. Dupont de Nemonrs and Company, the above equation for ROI has been expanded to suit decentralized operations, as under:

$$ROI = \frac{\text{Net operating income}}{\text{Net Sales}} \times \frac{\text{Net sales}}{\text{Net investment}}$$

Profit margin x capital turnover

Return on investment, thus, equals margin on sales multiplied by the turnover of capital. It, therefore, befits the divisional managers that they take the overall company view of returning a profit on the investment given at their command. This triangular structure of ROI *inter-alia* relationship tends to provide the managerial action plan. Profitability, can be increased either by stepping up the sales margin or the capital turnover or both the interesting facts. Thus, in a certain division, the ROI in year 1901 is 21%, with a sales margin of 7% and capital turnover of 3. If the management wants it to be increased to 28% in 1902, it is possible either through securing a higher turnover of 4 to assets keeping the margin, as before. The other way round is keeping the turnover at same 3, but having a higher mark up of 9.33%.

ROI is conceptually an appealing performance indicator in which it determines whether the division is profitable enough to support the amounts devoted to it. It makes possible comparison between divisions and alternate investments. It, further, draws on the neglected phase of idle resources in operations, which could be diverted, to other revenue generating opportunities.

However, ROI has its own limitations and shortcomings. It fails to consider the size of an investment, in that a small division with a high ROI may appear better than a larger division, when in fact, the opposite is true. It further distorts the behavioural pattern of the division manager. He may not launch fresh capital projects as the rate of return in the early stages of commercial production may be depressed. He might also abandon those older projects, which earn a rate of return of last equal to the cost of capital of the corporation, yet fail to meet the ROI standard. To boost this divisional return, if authority permits, he may go in for cheaper short-term sources of financing which will keep the investment base low. An additional gimmick that a clever manager might adopt is to base assets instead of purchasing them. He may structure many bases that the assets need not be capitalized and the divisions' investment base remains low. It were these weaknesses that led Dearden to observe "I believe that it is most important to get away from blindly using the ROI system and to develop procedures that best satisfy the requirements of each individual company. In, the management control field, I think we should recognize that ROI financial control was a very useful innovation when it was first developed, but that is now obsolete."

Divisional ROI

With a view to minimizing the above weaknesses and limitations, it has been suggested that the following formula be employed for computing the divisional ROI:

$$\frac{\text{Controllable revenue} - \text{Controllable costs}}{\text{Controllable capital employed}}$$

There are good reasons that the divisional manager should be judged only in terms of the elements which he can control. To hold him accountable for revenue and costs controllable by others will be injurious in as much as he is being held responsible for he has not been assigned.

But again, the question is of information reporting about the divisions. Unless, at least, some of the elements controllable by others are included within the calculation of divisional ROI, the return will be far away from the corporate return. Hence, it is suggested that the divisional performance should be evaluated in terms of "traceable" elements - those revenues and costs that could be identified with the profit making activities of the division.

Residual Income

Another accounting measure of profitability is the Residual Income (RI). It is the simple concept of absolute amount of earnings after a prescribed minimum charge in the invested capital. It is the rupee measure of profitability with a difference emphasising the marginal profit in rupees beyond a desired minimum rate of return. It is the residue of profit after having made a certain predator mind charge: This charge may represent either the cost of capital or target profit for the business segment. Symbolically,

RI = Reported Income – (Investment x charge rate)

if the invested capital in a certain corporation is Rs.85,00,000, the prescribed minimum capital charge has been taken at 12% and the income for the year has been reported as Rs.19,60,000, to:

RI = Rs.19,60,000 – (Rs,85,00,000 x 12 / 10)
= Rs.19,60,000 – Rs.10,20,000
= Rs. 9,40,000

It is not necessary that a common minimum charge is made for all segments. The charge may be kept different by the top management to recognize the unique identity and role of each segment in the overall company plan. Individual segment rates take care of such factors as maturity of the segment, its market position ad other situational considerations or the imputer interest rate. It is an opportunity or hypothetical cost rather than a real cost as no contractual lender borrower relationship exists, and no legal interest can be incurred. In a way, the capital charge resembles a separate application of central administrative overhead allocated to the decentralized division.

From the viewpoint of behavioral standpoint, RI is supposed to be superior to other measures. It meets the behavioral criteria of goal congruence, motivation, and anatomy better than other measures. After all, the goals of the corporate headquarters are no different from those of divisional manager crosses the hurdle test of a minimum capital levy, he should not be held back in his entrepreneurial efforts of going in for additional investments which are likely to improve the dollar/rupee profit of his associate or a subsidiary. Since RI is a rupee amount rather than a ratio, the particular division should expand as long as it maximizes the absolute income in excess of the desired minimum charge on investment. This explains the practical superiority and requirement of RI over ROI. The three distinct benefits of RI may be noted:

(i) Different rates of implied charges may be used for different types of assets warranting their risk-return trade-off

(ii) Requirement can be made that similar assets are imposed the same investment charge to make inter-period and intra-division comparisons meaningful.

(iii) Divisionalised growth is promoted because investments that exceed the opportunity cost of capital are encouraged.

Residual income, however, has its own conceptual problems. The first relates to the setting of the rate of capital charge. For instance, General Electric Inc., for many years, applied the imputed rate of 5%. But was it a fair figure in the fare of ever-increasing real and nominal interest rates and a representation of the cost of capital? Perhaps even the G.E. management was not convinced except that it continued using it on the grounds of uniformity and consistency. Second problem is that RI is not very understandable to the divisional managers. It becomes confusing to work with, as there is no simple answer as to which division is more successful at low rates of interest, but poorer at higher rates. It promotes favoritism towards the bigger divisions in ranking performance. Table 4.1 presents residual income statement for divisions of a multi corporation.

The larger the amount of investment, the more likely is the higher residual 'income'. Lastly, only a few major companies, making the inter-firm comparison extremely difficult, have adopted this criterion. These were the weaknesses, which finally persuaded the General Electric Corporation to abandon it in mid 1970s after several years of usage.

Multiple Criteria

As observed earlier, divisional performance measurement has many dimensions. Both profit and non-profit criteria have to be employed to evaluate what a division has really done. Very few chief executives would be happy with total reliance upon financial data as these may fail to expose the company's long-term strengths and weaknesses. Even among profit indicators there is no unique single criterion insufficient to judge as to how much a segment has contributed to the overall profitability.

Only a few corporations use a uni-divisional financial measure. The usual practice is to simultaneously use at least two measures, RI and ROI. The former serves as the minimum cut-off point in the case net present value approach to capital budgeting, the latter signifies the top management's target earning rate, which the decentralized divisions are expected to achieve with a view to confirming to organizational goals.

This is well evidenced by the survey of Reece and Cool, which reported that 30% of the firms in the U.S.A. used RI. Practically, all these firms also use ROI.

Standards and Point Assignments

Quantitative and qualitative measures, even if applied together fail to provide a sound basis for positive and negative incentives. The search is on far an adequate evaluation system, which incorporates both the financial and non-financial criteria, and applies it with standards and point assignments.

Table 4.1: Residual Income Statement for Divisions of a Multi Corporation

	Division 1 ($)	Division 2 ($)	Division 3 ($)	Total firm ($)
Revenue	5.960,000	1.345,000	9,087,000	16,392.000
Variable Costs	2.500.000	635.000	6.957.000	10,092.000
Contribution Margin	3.460,000	710,000	2.130,000	6.300.000
Discretionary Fixed Costs	1.500.000	100.000	530.000	2.130.000
Short-run performance margin	1.960,000	610,000	1.600,000	4.170.000
Traceable committed fixed costs	960.000	210.000	800.000	1.970.000
Segment Margin	1.000,000	400.000	800,000	2.200.000
Assignable Central Administration	100.000	40,000	80,000	220.000
*Investment charges	750.000	60.000	150.000	-0-
Residual Income	150,000	300.000	570,000	1,980.000
Non-assignable costs				694.000
Net income				1.286.000

*Minimum desired return 15% based upon asset book values of different division are as follows: $5.000.000 (div 1). $400.000 (div 2). $1.000.000 (div 3).

Transfer Pricing

The cost centres and profit centres are important to a decentralized organization because they help alleviate some of the difficulties of controlling diverse operations. Responsibility for a company's functions is placed with managers, and managers' performance is measured by comparing actual results with projected results.

Profit measurement and return on investment are important gauges of performance in decentralized divisions. But, at cost centres where only costs are involved, many people have difficulty measuring performance. This problem becomes more complicated when divisions within a company exchange goods or services and assume the role of customer or supplier to another division. This inter-division transfer of goods and services necessitates the use of transfer pricing. A transfer price is the price at which the goods are exchanged among a company's divisions. Such prices allow intra-company transactions to be measured and accounted for. These prices also affect the revenues and costs of the divisions involved. Furthermore, since a transfer price contains an estimated amount of profit, a manager's ability to meet a targeted profit can be measured. Although often called fictitious or created prices, company transfer prices as well as related policies are closely connected with performance evaluation.

Transfer Pricing Characteristics

The subject of transfer pricing is complex. Some scholars believe totally in the benefits of using transfer prices, while others hold these should never be used because these are not real prices. To illustrate how transfer prices are used and to help explain the difficult operational and behavioural aspects of such prices, we analyse two situations requiring them. Figure 4.1 is a pictorial view of how products flow at the Creative Pulp Company. This company is composed of three divisions: the Pulp Division, the Cardboard Division and the Box Division. Example 1 shows the pulp division transferring wood pulp to the cardboard division for

Figure 4.1: Intracompany Transfer Pricing Examples: Creative Pulp Company

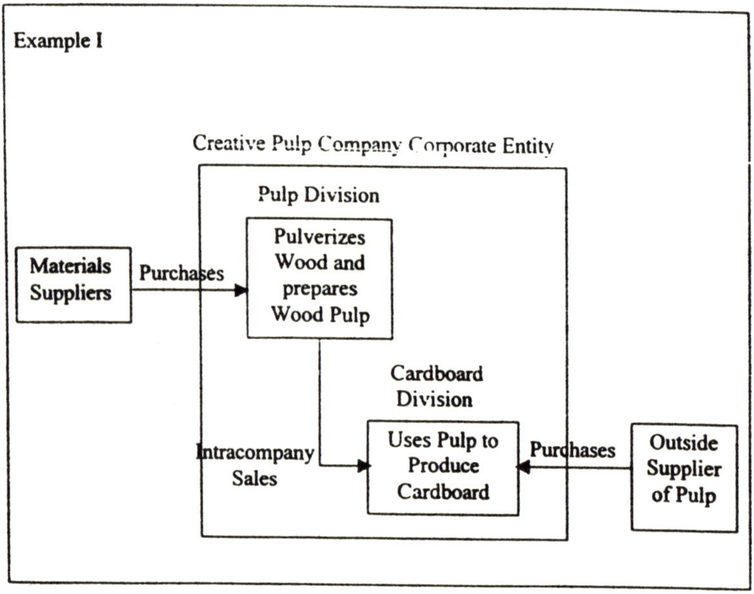

Figure 4.1: Intracompany Transfer Pricing Examples: Creative Pulp Company

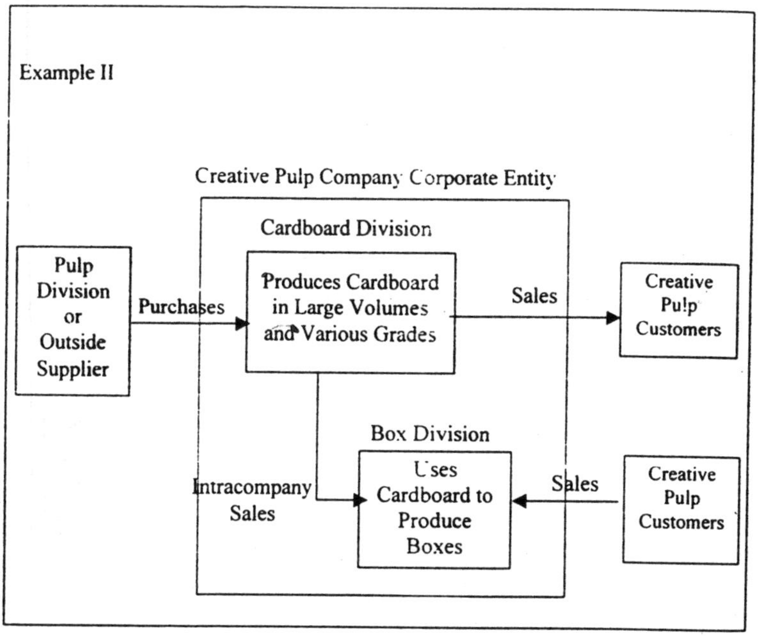

use in making cardboard. The cardboard division also has the option of purchasing the pulp from an outside supplier. The cost of making the pulp, including raw materials, labour, variable overhead and fixed overhead, is Rs.12.90 per kg. By adding a 10 per cent factor to cover miscellaneous and divisional overhead expenses as well as a small profit, the proposed transfer price amounts to Rs.14.19 per kg. The outside supplier will sell the pulp to the company for Rs.14.10 per kg. What should the manager of the Cardboard Division do in such situations?

Clearly, pressure is on the manager of the Pulp Division to lower the transfer price to an amount equal to or less than Rs.14.10, the market price. If this action is taken, the Rs.0.09 per kg reduction will directly affect profits of the Pulp Division. In turn, that situation will affect the manager's performance. On the other hand, if the manager of the Cardboard Division agrees to pay the Rs.14.19 per kg price to benefit performance evaluated on the basis of only budgeted and actual cost. But then, the overall company operating results, that person's profit and performance will be negatively affected. The question arises, either amount a fair price? Such a problem would not occur if costs were simply accumulated as the product travels through the production process. The Pulp Division could be treated as a cost centre and the manager's performance evaluated on the basis of only budgeted and actual costs. But the Pulp Division's return on investment could not be measured. These are the conflicting objectives of performance evaluation in a decentralized organization.

A second common situation is shown in Example-2 of Figure 4.1. Instead of an outside supplier influencing an internal transfer price, the Cardboard Division has an outside customer. The manager of the Cardboard Division must decide whether to sell cardboard to the outside customer at the rate of Rs.28.10 per kg. or to supply to the Box division at Rs.27.90 per kg. (Rs.27.90 covers all costs plus a profit margin).

Several problems that might arise must be considered. Is the outside customer going to make boxes that compete with the company's Box Division? Should the Box Division pay a market value transfer price so the Cardboard Division's manager can be evaluated properly? What about the Box Division? Should that manager suffer because managers of the Pulp and Cardboard Divisions have siphoned off all profits?

These are but some of the problems involved in using transfer prices. Perhaps one can now better understand why there are both proponents and opponents of this concept. It is easy to understand why transfer prices cause difference of opinion between managers. But measuring a manager's performance is still a major objective of decentralized companies, and the use of transfer prices is one important approach to that objective.

Transfer Pricing Methods

There are two primary approaches to develop a transfer price:

1. The price may be based on the cost of the item until its transfer to the next department or process.
2. A market value may be used if the item has an existing external market when transferred.

Both these pricing situations were present in the Creative Pulp Company illustration. There, the Pulp Division would be inclined to use the cost method sine no apparent outside market exists for the pulp product. The only user of pulp is the Cardboard Division. However, the Box Division will probably have to pay the market-related price for the cardboard since the Cardboard Division can either sell its product outside or transfer it to the Box Division.

In a situation in which no external markets are involved, divisional managers in a decentralized company may agree to a cost-plus transfer price or a negotiated transfer price. A cost-plus transfer price is the sum of costs incurred by the producing division plus an agreed-on profit percentage. The limitation of the cost-plus pricing is that cost recovery is guaranteed to the selling division, and guaranteed cost recovery fails to detect inefficient operating conditions as well as excessive cost incurrence. A negotiated transfer price, on the other hand, is bargained for by the managers of the buying and selling divisions. From the cost-plus side, a transfer price may be based on an agreement to use a standard cost plus a profit percentage. This approach emphasizes cost control through the use of standard costs while still allowing the selling division to return a profit even though it us a cost centre. A negotiated transfer price may also be based on a market price that was reduced in the bargaining process.

Market transfer prices are discussed but seldom used without being subjected to negotiations between managers. Using market prices may cause the selling division to ignore negotiation attempts from the buying division manager and sell directly to outside customers. If this causes an internal shortage of materials and forces the buying division to make a profit, such a use of market prices works against a company's overall operating objectives. Therefore, when market prices are used to develop transfer prices, they are normally used only as a basis of negotiation.

Developing a Transfer Price

Many of the normal pricing considerations are also present in the development of transfer price. The first step is to compute the unit of the item being transferred. Next, management must determine the appropriate profit mark-up. If the semi-finished product (i) has an existing market for the selling division to consider or (ii) can be purchased in similar condition by the buying division from an outside source, then the market price must be included in the analysis used to develop a transfer price. The final step is to have the managers negotiate a compromise between the two prices.

Now look again at the Creative Pulp Company example. The division manager's computations supporting the Rs.14.19 cost plus transfer price is shown in Table 4.2.

This one year budget is based on the expectation that the Cardboard Division will require 480,000 kgs. of pulp. Unit costs are stated in the right column. Notice that allocated corporate overhead is not included in the computation of the transfer price. Only costs related to the Pulp Division are included. The profit markup percentage of 10 percentage adds Rs.1.29 to the final transfer price of Rs.14.19.

Table 4.2: Transfer Price Computation
Creative Pulp Company
Pulp Division – Transfer Price Computation

Cost Category	Budgeted Costs	Cost per unit
Material		
Wood	Rs.1,584,000	Rs.3.30
Scrap wood	336,000	0.70
Labor		
Shaving/cleaning	768,000	1.60
Pulverizing	1,152,000	2.40
Blending	912,000	1.90
Overhead		
Variable	936,000	1.95
Fixed	504,000	1.05
Subtotals	Rs.6,192,000	Rs.12.90
Costs allocated from corporate Office	144,000	1.29
Target profit, 10% of division's costs	619,200	
Total costs and profit	Rs.6,955,200	
Cost plus transfer price		Rs.14.19

At this point, management could dictate that the unit Rs.14.19 be use. One the other hand, the manager of the Cardboard Division could bring the outside purchase price of Rs.14.19 per kg. to the attention of the management. Usually, such situations end up being negotiated to determine the final transfer price. Each side has a position and strong arguments to support a price. And each manager's performance will be compromised by adopting the other's price.

In the illustrations, both the managers bring their concerns to the attention of top management. A unique settlement is reached. Since internal profits must be erased before financial statements are prepared, management allows the Pulp Division to use the Rs.14.19 price and the Cardboard Division the Rs.14.10 price for purposes of performance evaluation. Obviously, the company does not want the Cardboard Division buying pulp from another company. At the same time, the Pulp Division has the right to a 10% profit. Such approaches are often used to maintain harmony within a corporation. In this case, it allows top management to measure the manager's performance while avoiding behavioral issues. The period over, all fictitious profits are cancelled by using adjusting entries before preparing end-of-year financial statements. The final product, in this case, has a profit factor that took into account all operations of the business.

Measuring Performance by Using Transfer Prices

When transfer prices are used, performance reports about managers of cost centres will contain revenue and income figures used in the evaluation. The Pulp Division performance report in Table 4.3 is a good example. The Pulp Division supplied 500 kgs. more of pulp than anticipated for the month. Sales were priced at Rs.14.19 per kg.

The variable costs per unit shown earlier were used to extend budgeted and actual amounts for materials, labor and variable overhead. The result was that the manager of the Pulp Division earned a March profit of Rs.43,350 which was Rs.1,170 over budgeted figure. The transfer price made it possible for the division to be evaluated as if it were a profit centre, even though the division does not sell to outside customers. Were the Pulp division still accounted for as a cost centre, the manager would have to explain costs being Rs.5,925 over budget instead of divisional income's being over target.

Conclusion

A typical business organization of today is growing larger and more complex. It is now a multi-product, multi-unit and multi-location entity with a number of decentralized divisions and subsidiaries.

Table 4.3: Performance Report using Transfer Prices

Creative Pulp Company

Pulp Division – Performance Report

	Budget (42,000 kgs)	Actual (42,500 kgs.)	Difference over / (under) Budget
Costs controllable by Supervisor	Rs.595,890	Rs.603,075	Rs.7,095
Sales to Cardboard Division			
Cost of Goods sold			
Materials			
Wood	Rs.138,600	Rs.140,250	Rs.1,650
Scrap Wood	29,400	29,750	350
Labor			
Shaving/cleaning	67,200	68,000	800
Pulverizing	100,800	102,000	1,200
Blending	79,800	80,750	950
Overhead			
Variable	81,900	82,875	975
Fixed	44,100	44,100	0
Total cost of goods sold	Rs.541,800	Rs.547,725	Rs.5,925
Gross margin from sales	Rs.54,180	Rs,55,350	Rs.1,170
Costs uncontrollable by Supervisor			
Cost allocated from Corporate Office	Rs.12,000	Rs.12,000	Rs. 0
Division's income	Rs.42,180	Rs.43,350	Rs,1,170

Most of the operating divisions have been investment centres rather than simple profit, revenue or cost centres. With this organizational structure, the all-important question is that of choosing an appropriate measure of performance evaluation. The four accepted financial measures are net income, contribution margin, return on investment, and residual income. The choice depends upon a number of economic and behavioral considerations. In practice, however, ROI and RI are simultaneously employed to support each other.

Thus, the problem of transfer price policy arises when Buying Division decides to purchase from outside suppliers. A Selling Division with adequate capacity to fulfil the Buying Division's demands should sell to that division at any price that recovers incremental costs. Incremental costs of intra-company sales include all variable costs of production and distribution plus any fixed costs directly traceably to intra-company sales. If a buying division can acquire products from outside suppliers at an actual cost that is less than the supplying division's incremental costs, then, purchases should be made from the outside supplier because overall company profits will be enhanced.

Notes

1. Shillinglaw, Gordon, "Cost Accounting, Analysis and Control" (Homewood III. Richard D, Irwin, 1972), pp 547-48.

5

Transfer Pricing – International Legislations and Standards

Transfer pricing remains a key international tax issue for MNCs. Tax and financial executives worldwide are under pressure to resolve the complex business and transfer pricing matter brought on by the globalisation of their organisation and the growing cadre of aggressive revenue authorities. Globally, more than 60% of the world trade takes place within MNCs. [1] Most of the MNCs, in order to reduce their global tax cost, tend to shift profit from a high tax jurisdiction to a low tax jurisdiction, which consequently leads to shift of tax revenues. To this end, the advanced countries have made relevant legislative provisions. The provisions made by these countries form the subject matter of this chapter. About one third of this chapter is devoted to the practices followed by different countries and, the rest discusses the legislation and standards issued by selected developed countries in the recent past.

Transfer Pricing – Global Practices

From a business perspective, there are many dimensions to deciding what to charge for the inter-company exchange of goods and services. Compensation and performance measurement may push in one direction; the demand for simplicity may push in another; and tax considerations may push in a third. Other factors may come into play as well. Governments, through their tax systems, have a vested interest in ensuring that appropriate profits are reported in their jurisdiction. Government concerns are heightened when one of the parties to a related party transaction is subject to tax at a rate that is considerably less than that applying in the other related party's country. In addition to tax-rate pressures, other government pressures can be brought to bear on the transfer pricing decision, including heavy penalties or restrictive measures dealing with related-party transactions.

There is a general agreement among governments, often by way of bilateral tax treaties that transfer pricing between related parties should carry out related transactions between themselves on the same basis as would have applied had they not been related. [2] Through the Organization for Economic Cooperation and Development (OECD) 25 of the world's leading industrialized countries, including Canada, have stated their acceptance of the arm's length standard for setting inter-company transfer prices and have set out guidelines for methods that should be used in adhering to the standard. [3]

Notwithstanding this agreement on the arm's length standard, various countries have different ways of interpreting the standard and applying the generally accepted methods. [4] It is these differences that cause uncertainty and introduce tax risk to the equation. An MNC is then left to balance the conflicting interpretations in a manner that exposes it to the least amount of financial risk. This determination is affected by the geographic source of the greatest volume of transactions. A U.S. based MNC will likely to have more related-party transactions to be reported in the U.S. than in any other single country, and therefore its tax risk is likely to be more significant in the U.S. than in any other country. It is also affected by the existence of tax and other financial penalties.

The attitude of MNCs to the transfer pricing policies and administrative procedures developed by various governments has been the subjects of four Ernst and Young surveys in the past years. [5] The survey conducted in 1995 concentrated on various aspects of transfer pricing development. The focus of 1996 survey was on transfer pricing documentation. The focus of 1997 and 1999 Surveys was on practices, perceptions and trends of transfer pricing in different countries.

Ernst and Young Global Survey [6] – 1995

In 1995, Ernst and Young International arranged for an independent survey of multinational companies operating in eight countries namely the U.S., Canada, Australia, France, Germany, the Netherlands and the U.K. [7] The Survey also asked the tax authorities in the surveyed countries to comment on various aspects of the transfer pricing developments and the use of advance pricing agreement (APAs). [8] The results of this survey establish the following:

- Transfer pricing is vitally important to MNCs in all surveyed countries,
- The more MNCs are subject to tax audit on transfer pricing methods, the more they take reactions of tax authorities into account when establishing or revising TPMs, and
- Most MNCs are familiar with the concept of APAs, and expect their Use to increase in future.

In the survey 80 % of MNCs indicated that transfer pricing was the most important international tax issue facing them today. Approximately one half of all respondents deposed it was the most pressing tax issue of any kind for them. [9] Overall 83 percentage of respondents indicated that their TPMs had attracted tax authority review.

When asked about audits of their foreign subsidiaries, MNCs uniformly identified the United States as most active in conducting transfer pricing audits; Canada was well down the list. 36 % of Canadian respondents indicated that they are facing a review by a foreign tax authority, 34% of all MNCs that have faced an enquiry in subsidiary country report that they are currently under review by the IRS of U.S. and 34% report they have been reviewed by the IRS (U.S.) in the past, for Canada, the figures are 12% and 11% respectively.

It was further observed in the survey that the chief reason for this consideration is strict U.S. regulations and penalty regime (over 90% of U.S. MNCs are likely to design TPM keeping in mind the observations of IRS, the Canadian (88%) and U.K. (84%)) MNCs closely followed the U.S. in this regard. Even in Germany and France, where the tax authorities are less aggressive in reviewing TPMs, just over 70% of respondents considered the prospect of review significant enough to take it into account in setting TPMs.

Larger MNCs treated the risk (possibility of review by revenue authorities) more seriously than the smaller ones. Companies that had experienced revenue enquiries in the past were more likely to take the risk into account than those companies that had not faced such inquiries. [10] Further, approximately one third of respondents claimed that they set up a defensible policy with adequate supporting documentation. Almost one third adapted their TPMs to the practice of local tax authorities. Only one quarter stated that they use an arm's length market based approach. A number of MNCs also indicated that they tailor TPMs to the more conservative approach of certain countries, most notably the United States. [11] The particular mention of U.S. rules seems to support the fear of other countries, including Canada, that U.S. rule and penalty provisions have caused MNCs to skew their TPMs to 'over comply' with the U.S. rules. [12]

As regards the types of transactions that come under review, MNCs identified the transaction in the following order:-

- Charges for administrative or management services
- Royalties and other charges for intangibles
- Transfer pricing for goods for resale
- Financing transactions
- Charges for technical services

Needless to say administrative and management charges are the easiest for the revenue authorities to trace and audit. For these charges, the three part audit determination of existence, benefit and non-duplication accompanied by a "no-mark up" approach make it easy for the author to assess reasonability of the charges. [13]

According to the information obtained from the Inland Revenue System (IRS), transfer pricing for goods or intangibles is somewhat more difficult to evaluate and is open to more subjective judgement in many cases. Nonetheless, various unpublished Canadian surveys indicate that their auditors are increasingly willing to look at goods and royalties when auditing international transactions. In the United States, while interest and royalties are the most frequently adjusted transactions, the dollar adjustments for transfer of goods are larger.

The survey also covered competent authority procedures. Respondents were generally dissatisfied with the competent authority process, 52% in Canada, generally due to the amount of time involved, many years, and the uncertainty as to the outcome of the process. To some extent this was mirrored by comments on the APA process. Despite the current lack of use of APAs by Canadian-based MNCs, almost all of them were familiar with the APA concept and some 80% of them expected the use of APAs to increase in the future. [14]

Ernst and Young Survey of Transfer Pricing Documentation – 1996 [15]

Recognizing the importance of transfer pricing and the growing compliance burden for documenting transfer pricing policies, particularly for U.S. purposes, Ernst and Young sought responses from MNCs on these vital issues. Responses were received from over 200 MNCs, 90% of which were based in the United States. As was the case for the 1995 survey, transfer pricing was identified as the major tax concern facing MNCs.

Almost 90% of the respondents indicated that the reasons for documenting their transfer pricing policies included the objective of minimising exposure to U.S. penalties. Almost two-thirds of them indicated that they documented the facts in anticipation of an IRS audit and half of them were seeking an evaluation of their transfer pricing exposure. Slightly more than 40% of the respondents were attempting to substantiate their methodology for non-U.S. purposes. Almost three quarters of the respondents indicated that their documentation included all or most of the documentation required under the U.S. transfer pricing regulations.

The respondents made it clear that they were less concerned about non-U.S. documentation requirement: one third indicated that they would not prepare documentation for foreign tax authorities. Approximately, one half said they would use U.S. documentation for foreign purposes, mostly without modification. Only one in four indicated that they would prepare separate documentation for foreign purposes. This response is, perhaps, attributable to the lack of documentation requirements and the lack of meaningful penalties in most countries.

Despite the fact that the use of a results-based comparable profits method [16] (CPM) is generally resisted by other countries [17], 49% of respondents use this method, along or in combination with another method, for pricing the transfer of goods, while 37% use it for intangibles. Approximately one half of the respondents used more than one method for pricing goods, and one quarter used more than one method for intangibles. Since use of CPM is not accepted by the OECD [18] without reservation, the extent to which it is used by the respondents indicates the impact of the detailed U.S. regulations and penalties on the transfer pricing decision. This influence was recognised by many of the respondents; 25% of those using CPM expected to recast CPM for foreign purposes as another method and 10% of those using CPM expected to be challenged in foreign jurisdictions. Some 40 % were unsure of the impact of using CPM, and 25% expected no foreign difficulties.

Approximately one half of respondents were under audit in their transfer pricing policies, and many had been asked to supply documentation by foreign jurisdictions, as shown below in Table 5.1.

The results confirmed Canada's increased activity in this area and its diligence in seeking documentation, despite the absence of legislative or regulatory documentation requirements or penalties.

The survey also found that over 60% of respondents used external advisors in the process of completing their documentation requirements. The costs of completing these requirements were relatively high, whether in dollars expended or in person hours, as illustrated in Table 5.2.

Table 5.1: Companies under Audit in Selected Countries

Country	No. Under audit	No. asked to supply documents
Canada	28	16
United Kingdom	24	7
Germany	13	3
Australia	10	8
United States	19	n/a
Other	22	11

Table 5.2: Cost of Compliance

Sales Volume (US $)	Median Cost (US $)	Median hours
< 500 million	45,000	120
500 million to 1 billion	50,000	165
1 to 5 billion	100,000	200
> 5 billion	150,000	500

The amounts expended, in both dollars and in time, were higher for non-U.S. companies than for the U.S. based MNCs. The above table illustrates that the costs of compliance fall relatively more heavily on smaller companies.

Ernst and Young Survey of Transfer Pricing Documentation, 1997 and 1999

In 1997, Ernst and Young commissioned a landmark global survey on transfer pricing practices, perceptions and trends in 12 countries. Nearly 400 multinational parent companies, more than 70 subsidiaries of foreign owned parents in the United States and Europe, and numerous tax authorities and tax specialists were interviewed. Countries included in the 1997 survey were: Australia, Canada, France, Germany, Italy, Japan, Korea, the Netherlands, Sweden, Switzerland, the United Kingdom and United States. In 1999, they expanded the 1997 survey from the

12 primary countries to also include Argentina, Brazil, Denmark, Finland, Mexico, Norway and Spain. Close to 600 tax and finance directors in multinational parent companies were interviewed. In addition, 124 interviews were conducted with subsidiaries of leading multinational companies in Canada, Europe, Mexico and the United States. They also gathered insights from revenue authorities and tax specialties in all 19 surveyed countries. Table 5.3 presents highlights of the global surveys of 1999 and 1997.

Legislation and Standards in Select Developed Countries

(a) Organisation for Economic Cooperation and Development (OECD)

Transfer Pricing Guidelines

OECD, founded in Paris in December 1960, endeavoured to arrive at a consensus on international taxation principles, thereby avoiding unilateral responses to multilateral problems. It has issued detailed transfer pricing guidelines, "Transfer Pricing for Multinational Enterprises and Tax Administration" for multinational enterprises in 1979, which were revised in 1995("OECD Report"). The OECD report is considered as authoritative statement on the subject.

Overview

The basic principle reflected in the OECD guidelines is that arm's length prices should be used in all intra-group transactions.

Prescribed and Preferred Methods

OECD has prescribed CUP, RPM, CPM, PSM and TNMM methods as the means for determination of the arm's length price. However, the guidelines suggest that transaction based methods are preferable over profit-based methods. The Indian Regulations are consistent with the OECD guidelines in this regard.

Table 5.3: Global Survey Highlights

1997 Survey Highlights	1999 Survey Highlights
• MNCs throughout the world regard transfer pricing as the most important international tax issue their organisations will face over the next two years.	• MNCs throughout the world increasingly regard transfer pricing as the most important international tax issue their organisations will face over the next two years. The proportion of MNCs citing transfer pricing as the most important issue grew from 52% in 1997 to 61% in the 1999 survey
• By an even larger majority, subsidiaries of MNCs regard transfer pricing as their most important tax issue. Indeed, eight of ten MNC subsidiaries cited transfer pricing as the most important international tax issue they will face over the next two years.	• By an overwhelming majority, subsidiaries of MNCs regard transfer pricing as their most important tax issue. Indeed 97% of MNC subsidiaries cited transfer pricing as the most important international tax issue they will face over the next two years.
• Nearly two thirds of MNCs surveyed report their inter-company transactions have	• Nearly two-thirds of MNCs headquartered in the 12 countries included in the 1997 survey, this

already been the target of a tax authority examination	year reports their inter-company transactions have already been the target of a tax authority examination. A smaller number of (about 40%) of MNCs headquartered in the seven countries added to the 1999 survey report, that their transfer pricing has been the subject of a tax authority examination.
• On average, there is a one-in-two chance of defending profits in a transfer pricing enquiry anywhere in the world	• Once again, there is a one-in-two chance of defending profits in a transfer pricing enquiry anywhere in the world. Of those reporting adjustments, 42 % said that transfer pricing adjustments resulted in double taxation.
• Eight in ten multinationals expect to face a transfer pricing examination within the next two years	• As was the case in the 1997 survey, eight in ten MNCs expect to face a transfer pricing examination within the next two years.
• Inter-company services are considered	• Inter-company services continue to be

by MNCs the most susceptible to transfer pricing disputes worldwide	viewed by MNCs as the transactions most susceptible to transfer pricing disputes worldwide.
• Transfer pricing is viewed as a compliance exercise in a majority of organizations. It has made the move to the boardroom as an integral part of corporate strategic planning in only about one-quarter of the MNCs surveyed	• Despite the growing importance of transfer pricing, the percentage of companies making it an integral part of planning has not increased since the 1997 survey. Instead, a majority of companies tend to view it largely as a compliance exercise. However, tax and finance executives believe the upfront involvement of transfer pricing in strategic decisions could help maximise operating performance and reduce the global tax burden.
• MNCs identify maximization of operating performance, not optimizing tax arrangements, as the most important factor in shaping transfer pricing policies	• MNCs continue to identify maximization of operating performance, not optimizing tax arrangements, as the most important factor in shaping transfer pricing policies. In fact, out of five factors listed, optimizing tax results was fourth

	down the list
• MNCs are struggling to understand what kind of transfer pricing documentation is required of them. In the absence of clear local guidelines, MNCs are documenting according to strict U.S. rules.	• MNCs increasingly recognize the advantages of an integrated global documentation approach, but few have achieved this goal.
• MNCs tend to use transaction-based pricing methods more often than profit-based methods.	• MNCs continue to use transaction-based pricing methods more often than profit-based methods, despite the difficulty of defending them on audit.
• APA processes outside the United States are not well understood by the MNC community nor are they particularly well defined by fiscal authorities.	• APA processes are becoming better understood around the world. Whereas in 1997 more companies indicated that they would not consider using an APA than would, they reverse is the case for the 1999 survey, more said they would consider using an APA than would not.

• Many fiscal authorities in both developed and emerging markets are paying increased attention to transfer pricing compliance.	• Tax authorities have increased cross-border dialogues and transfer pricing enforcement abilities.

Penalty

The guidelines prescribe levy of penalty ranging from 10% to 200% of the additional tax. It suggests partial relief where the taxpayers are able to prove its bonafide.

Documentation and Disclosures

Limited information has been prescribed to be furnished at the time of filling of the tax return. The tax return should contain information that would allow revenue authorities to determine the requirement for tax audit. Detailed information is required to be provided only in cases of audit. In contrast, the Indian regulations require a fairly detailed information statement to be filed with the return of income.

(b) U.S.A.

Overview

U.S. taxation is governed by the Internal Revenue Code (IRC), which is administered by the Internal Revenue Service (IRS). The IRS has been granted broad discretionary authority under section 482 of the Code to reallocate income, the deductions and other tax items among commonly controlled entities that do not deal with one another on arm's length terms.

The U.S.A. was first to introduce transfer pricing regulations way back in 1968 and has adopted the arm's length standard. The 1968 regulations formed the basis for the 1979 Report of the OECD Committee on Fiscal Affairs and the detailed pricing rules of several other countries e.g., Canada, Germany and Japan.

The IRS issued new revised transfer pricing regulations in 1994. The revised regulations provide specific methods to determine whether transactions between or among members of a controlled group satisfy the arm's length nature of the controlled transactions by reference to comparable transactions between uncontrolled parties. Generally, restructuring is exempt from transfer pricing regulations.

Acceptance and Priority Methods

U.S.A. recognizes CUP, RPM, CPM, comparable profit split and residual profit split methods. The choice of method is left to the assessee.

In selecting a method, the two primary factors to consider are the degree of comparability between the controlled and uncontrolled transactions and the quality of data and assumptions. In determining whether controlled and uncontrolled transactions are comparable, one must compare:

- The functions performed and resources employed by the controlled and uncontrolled taxpayers
- The significant contractual terms that could affect the prices charges on the profit earned in the two transactions
- The risks borne in each transaction
- The significant economic factors that could affect prices or profit in the two transactions viz. geographical market, level of the market, competition and location savings
- The property or services involved in the transactions

Advance Pricing Agreements

In order to reduce controversies over inter-company pricing, the IRS has issued provisions, which permit a taxpayer to seek an advance pricing agreements (APA). An APA covers the application of transfer pricing methodology to certain international transactions of foreign or domestic taxpayers.

An APA is a binding agreement between a taxpayer and the IRS. If the taxpayer complies with the terms of the APA, the pricing methodology proposed by the APA will be considered as satisfying the arm's length standard.

The 1994 regulations and the contemporaneous documentation requirements of the legislation have also led taxpayers to consider APAs. There are stiff penalties for failure to keep these records if a transfer pricing adjustments is made.

Penalty

U.S.A. laws provide levy of penalty @20% or 40% of the additional tax arising on account of transfer pricing adjustments. However, no penalty is levied if the pricing method is reasonably applied and documented.

Documentation and Disclosures

The final regulations set out the following ten principal documents necessary to support the use of the best method. [19]

- An overview of the taxpayer's business, including economic and legal factors affecting pricing
- A description of corporate structure affecting related-party transactions
- Supporting documents and agreements
- Description of the selected transfer pricing methods(TPMs) and reasons for selecting them
- Description of rejected methods and reasons for rejecting them
- Descriptions and analyses of related party transactions
- Descriptions and analyses of comparables used to support the choices made
- Explanation of economic analysis and projections
- A description of relevant data obtained between the end of the year and the time the tax return was filed and
- A general index of principal supporting documents

In addition, contemporaneous documentation, must be available but need not be filed with the tax returns, the IRS requires that certain information on related-party transactions and off shore activities be included when filling. [20]

Time Limit for Adjustment

The time limit for making any adjustment on account of transfer pricing is three years from the due date of filing return or actual filing date, whichever is later. However, in case of substantial understatements of tax, period is doubled. Where no return is filed, the period is unlimited.

(c) United Kingdom

Overview

Section 770(1) of the U.K. tax law empowers the Inland Revenue, by specific direction, to adjust the taxable income or gain of any company within the charge to U.K. tax arising from a non-arm's length transaction with a U.K. or overseas connected party. There is no further legislative or regulatory guidance as to what constitutes an arm's length price.

Section 770(1) (as extended by section 773(4) is sufficiently broad to catch virtually all inter-company transactions in goods, services, intangible assets and other facilities (including transactions of a financial nature).

Acceptable and Priority Methods

The only official guideline as to what constitutes an arm's length price appears in the form of revenue guidance notes. These notes essentially follow the approach adopted in the OECD Report.

The Inland Revenue approach to determining "the arm's length price" is highly pragmatic and recognizes that there is no single, universally flawless method or figure in any given set of circumstances.

Advance Transfer Pricing

APA mechanism similar to the one prevailing in the U.S.A. is available. However, the mechanism is generally restricted to major litigate areas.

Penalty

Any failure to compute profits on arm's length basis and to comply with documentation requirement could attract penalty up to 100% of the additional tax. However, no penalty is levied if the assessee has acted bonafide and has evidence to demonstrate the same.

Documentation and Disclosures

The burden to demonstrate reasonable pricing is on the assessee. Accordingly, the assessee is required to maintain appropriate records in support thereof. Further, there is prescribed documentation to support the method selected, comparables, etc. Taxpayers are expected to maintain document contemporaneously. There are no separate disclosures requirements.

Time Limit for Adjustment

The time limit for making any adjustment on account of transfer pricing is six years from the end of the accounting year.

(d) Japan

Overview

Japan's transfer pricing rules are part of the "Special Tax measures Law". The rules are triggered when a transaction is done between a Japanese juridical person and foreign affiliated person for consideration that was different from an arm's length price and that resulted in a reduction of taxable income in Japan.

Transactions will be within the scope of Japan's transfer pricing law only if a domestic person and a foreign affiliated person" are involved. The rules are limited to judicial persons and selected other entities but do not apply to transactions in which one of the parties is an individual.

Transactions, between a head office and branch would fall outside the scope of the transfer pricing rules, although the methods used to allocate income between such components of a single juridical entity resemble those applied in the transfer pricing context.

Transactions between a domestic persons and a foreign affiliated person that has a permanent establishment are excluded from the scope of the transfer pricing rules to the extent that the foreign affiliated person is taxable in Japan on the income arising from that transaction.

In the event that an unrelated entity is interposed between a domestic person and a foreign affiliated person, the transactions between the domestic person and that unrelated entity may be deemed to be one coming within the scope of the transfer pricing rules.

Acceptable and Priority of Methods

Japan recognizes CUP, RPM, CPM and other method, such as PSM. Alike United Kingdom, transaction-based methods are preferred to profit-based methods.

Pre-confirmation

The tax administration authority has introduced the "pre-confirmation" system similar to the advance pricing agreement procedure in the United States. To date, however, the disclosure requirements have proven so time-consuming and otherwise burdensome that only a few pre-confirmations have been successfully concluded in Japan. The pre-confirmation must contain the following:

- A description of the method that is proposed as the most reasonable method for calculating arm's length price for the transaction
- Data corroborating that the proposed method is the most reasonable method. Data submitted with the request should clearly describe the subject transaction, the comparable transactions upon which the arms length price is based and necessary adjustments to compensate for differences.

Penalty

There are no specific provisions dealing with penalties under the transfer pricing provisions. Accordingly, the general provisions apply. General rate of penalty is 10% on the additional tax plus additional 5% on the excess of deficiency tax over the tax as per return. There is no provision for relaxation from levy of penalty.

Documentation and Disclosures

There are no statutory provisions prescribing maintenance of documents. However, documents in support of method selected, comparables, and economic analysis are generally called for. The regulations require detailed statement concerning foreign affiliated persons.

Time Limit for Adjustment

The time limit for making any adjustment on account of transfer pricing is six years from the due date of filing of return.

(e) Germany

Germany has adopted the OECD approach to inter-company transactions. In 1983, the German tax administration had issued "Administration Principles", which contain the administrative guidelines for determining what constitutes "arm's length" *vis-à-vis* business transactions among related parties. The guidelines were revised on 24th December 1999 by two decrees commenting on taxation of income and property of permanent establishments and inter-corporate assessment between international related enterprises on 30th December. While the administration principles are not formally a part of the German tax law, and thus not legally binding for the taxpayer, these principles are not binding on the tax administration. As such, the administration principles provide a type of safe haven for tax planners and offer the taxpayer a number of arguments that could be employed against a tax auditor.

Advance Transfer Pricing

There are no formal APA procedures. German taxpayers may apply for such a ruling if they do not intend to receive an official certificate under a tax saving scheme, and provided that the ruling is requested for an intended future and not for an already implemented structure. Safe harbour rules are relatively unknown in German tax law, at least as far as inter-company pricing is concerned.

Accepted and Priority of Methods

Germany recognizes CUP, RAM and CPM methods. As in United Kingdom and Japan, transaction-based methods are preferred over profit-based methods.

Penalty

There are no penalties prescribed under the current law.

Documentation and Disclosures

There are no statutory provisions prescribing maintenance of documents. However, documents in support of method selected, comparables, etc. are generally called for. There are no separate disclosure requirements.

Time Limit of Adjustment

The time limit for making any adjustment on account of transfer pricing is four years from the date of filing of the income. In case of fraud, the period is ten years.

(f) Australia

In addition to supporting and expanding the use of APAs, the Australian Taxation Office (ATO) has issued comprehensive transfer pricing rules. The ATO has also issued draft tax rulings, which outline its position on the following:

- Selection and application of transfer pricing methodologies
- Documentation requirements
- Penalties for non-compliance

The ATO has expanded its tax audit and tax strategy review program by conducting transfer pricing risk-assessment reviews that comprise a very specific and detailed review of a taxpayer's transfer pricing practices. The ATO has set out its guidelines as to how taxpayers should evaluate their exposure to penalties and their risk of transfer pricing adjustments.

The ATO bases its penalty regime on two criteria: first, whether the taxpayer had a dominant purpose of tax avoidance and secondly, whether the taxpayer has a reasonably arguable position regarding compliance with the arm's length principle. The rates of penalty vary generally between 10% and 50 % of the tax adjustment, but are more commonly between 10% and 25 % where there is no purpose of tax avoidance. The ATO has a residual discretion to remit transfer pricing penalties.

The ATO expects that all taxpayers will create and maintain contemporaneous documentation of their TPMs. This documentation should include the following:

- Documents created in the ordinary course of business
- A functional analysis
- Support for the method chosen
- Documents prepared in the course of review of the TPM

The ATO requires that taxpayers complete a reporting form outlining the nature and extent of transactions between related. [21]

(g) Brazil

The Brazilian government released a transfer pricing regulation on May 5 that will require taxpayers in some situations to apply a form of formulatory apportionment in setting transfer prices due to the use of arbitrary, government-determined profit margins for certain related-party transactions.

The Brazilian transfer pricing regulation combines elements of the arm's length principle with elements of formulary apportionment. The regulation also differs from those adopted by many tax authorities in that there are separate sets of pricing methods for inbound transactions and for outbound transactions. The regulation was published on May 5 in the Diario Official da Uniao, Brazil's version of the U.S. Federal Register. The regulation implements transfer pricing legislation that took effect on Jan 1, 1997, that gave the government broad authority to adjust profit margins from related-party transactions (5 transfer pricing report 529, 1/1/1997).

The transfer pricing regulation will apply to related-party transactions as of January 1, 1997 but will not be applied retroactively. Brazilian taxpayers had been concerned that the regulation would apply to open years.

Pricing Methods

For property, services, and rights acquired from outside Brazil, the regulation calls for use of either the:

- Comparable uncontrolled profit method
- Resale price less profit method
- Cost plus method

For outbound transactions, Brazil's regulation requires use of either

- The export sales price method
- The wholesale price in the country of destination less profit method
- The acquisition or production cost plus taxes and profit method

Aspects of the Brazilian transfer pricing regulation diverge from the arm's length principle. Most notably, the resale and cost plus methods in the regulation have arbitrary profit margins, which are statutorily set by the government and are provided for the taxpayer to arrive at "arm's length" prices. Depending on the selected transfer pricing method, this process of computing prices may resemble more a formulary approach than an arm's length standard that is based on the analysis of facts and circumstances surrounding each individual situation.

Other Profit Margins

The profit margins are set between 15% and 30% depending on the transfer pricing method. The margins differ, depending on whether the related-party transactions are inbound or outbound. There is no justification in the regulations why profit margins derived from uncontrolled comparables cannot be used as the general rule.

The regulation allows use of different profit margins than those pre-established in the regulation, but the taxpayer must go through an intricate administrative process to do so. The taxpayer must provide additional documentation to justify what should be the correct arm's length profit margin for the taxpayer's specific situation and then wait for government approval.

The methods do not distinguish between tangible and intangible property or between services and property. The transfer pricing methods refer to the comparison or reconstruction of prices. The regulation would exclude use of profit splits or other profit-based methods, such as the transactional net margin methods (TNMM) or the comparable profit method (CPM). The concept of 'transactional pricing' is taken literally by the Brazilian tax authorities. In practical terms, the taxpayer is left with two real options: to use some sort of comparable uncontrolled price-retail or wholesale price observed in Brazil or abroad, or construct its transfer price based on its production or acquisition costs, cost plus method.

Arm's Length Principle

The Brazilian regulation somewhat follows OECD revised transfer pricing guidelines issued in 1994 and 1995. For example, the regulation endorses, although not explicitly, the arm's length principle in setting transfer prices.

The regulation will further allow taxpayers some compliance leeway by not imposing a transfer pricing adjustment if the taxpayer's transfer prices fall within 5% of the actual figures contained in import and export documents. The regulation will not apply to royalty payments, technical assistance, and scientific and administrative fees. These payments remain subject to the deductibility conditions contained in other legislation.

The Brazilian rule also does not require the tax payer to demonstrate that it has selected the most accurate and reliable method available, based on the facts and circumstances – similar to the U.S. best method rule. However, if the taxpayer uses more than one method, it may use the method that provides the more favorable results.

For the first time, Brazilian taxpayers will have specific guidelines on standards of comparability. Prior to release of the regulation, the only factor for determining comparability present in the regulations was similarity in contractual terms. There was no mention of comparability adjustments. The latest regulation will allow adjustments for factors that affect comparability, including:

- Payment terms
- Volume
- Payment guarantees
- Marketing and advertising expenses
- Costs related to quality control and hygienic standards
- Intermediate costs in buying and selling operations
- Packing
- Freight and insurance costs
- Physical property and content
- Unusual commodity price variations
- Export credit risk

Safe Harbours

The transfer pricing regulation also provides two types of safe harbours for outbound transactions. The first safe harbour provides that there will be no transfer pricing adjustment when the average export price of products, services, or right is equal to greater than 90% of the average sale price charged for the same products, services, or rights in the Brazilian market during the same time period and with similar payment terms.

Under the second safe harbour, officials will waive transfer pricing disclosure requirements if the taxpayer demonstrates that it derived a net profit from export sales to affiliates of at least 5% of its total related party export revenue. The computation of the 5% figure must not include social security contributions and income taxes. However, if the taxpayer can show that its net export revenue has never exceeded 5% of the total net revenue reported in the same time period, tax authorities also will waive disclosure requirements.

Brazilian officials acknowledge that use of safe harbors runs counter to OECD guidelines. However, government officials take the position that the drawbacks of using safe harbours may be outweighed by anticipated benefits, such as simplified taxpayer compliance and administrative relief for tax officials.

In a provision aimed at tax heaven the Brazilian regulation will automatically assume that any transaction with companies located in tax heavens is not at arm's length – similar to language adopted by the Mexican government. Moreover, if a Brazilian company completes a transaction with a company located in a tax heaven, officials will automatically treat the transaction as a related-party action and apply the transfer pricing regulation, regardless of whether the two companies are affiliated.

Market Penetration

In addition, the regulation will allow a taxpayer to adopt market penetration strategies that adopt lower than usual prices for comparable products, services, or rights if the taxpayer is entering a new market. A market penetration strategy will be taken into account only if the taxpayer provides supporting documentation that substantiates its strategy – including a government approved export plan, adding that a market penetration strategy can be pursued for maximum of 12 months.

The government also imposed other restrictions that will likely limit use of a market penetration strategy. For example, a Brazilian affiliate located abroad must sell in its local market its imported products, including those from a Brazilian parent, at a price that is below the prevailing market prices. However, this could trigger a price dumping case by the local competitors in that affiliate's market.

In addition, the regulation provides a broad definition of a controlled party, saying control includes situations when at least 10% of the capital stock of each entity belongs to the same individual or juridical entity. The regulation expands even further the definition of a controlled entity to include any distributor, agent or concessionaire that holds exclusive distribution rights for a specific territory in the country of destination, in the case of exports, or in Brazil, in the case of imports.

The new regulation could result in dramatic changes in the way Brazilians handle transfer pricing issues. Until recently, transfer pricing in Brazil was comprised of a set of laws, presidential decrees, and normative acts designed to curb the potential for a disguised distribution of profits by subsidiaries of foreign corporations operating in Brazil. There were no transfer pricing methods, guidelines or regulations, and enforcement was virtually non-existent.

(h) Canada

A number of important developments have taken place in Canada. Revenue in Canada has become more visible in reviewing international transactions. It is apparent that several district offices are selecting companies for audit on the basis of their R-106 forms themselves have been expanded for filing after 1995. Penalties have also been increased for non-compliance, but generally are limited to $ 48000 in extreme cases. Routine cyclical audits frequently involve referrals to international specialists within the local tax service office (TSO). Furthermore, some TSOs specialize in particular industries. Unlike the IRS in U.S., Revenue Canada TSOs, do not appear to have ready access to local economists and process engineers; however, the international division in Ottawa does have an Economic Analysis Group that provides support to the TSOs.

Until recently, the majority of Revenue Canada audits would focus on inter-company service charges. These audits would generally follow a predictable pattern: a request for foreign based information, a proposal to travel, at the taxpayer's expense, to the foreign location to examine its books and records, and a request for a functional analysis and for interviews with foreign personnel. If the requested information is not submitted, Revenue Canada may invoke Section 231.6 of the Income Tax Act to obtain foreign-based information relevant to the determination of a Canadian taxpayer's income.

In the past, audits would often result in a partial disallowance of inter-company charges and the use of subsection 15(1) or (2) to assess the non-resident parent as well. Queries relating to transfer pricing for tangible goods or intangibles were somewhat rare. That has now changed. Field auditors now routinely ask for functional analysis to support TPMs for tangible goods; as well, royalties are under review. Increasingly, the auditor will rely on information obtained from other audits as guidelines in determining whether a particular pricing approach gives results within a reasonable range.

Looking ahead, it is possible that revenue Canada auditors will start asking for copies of the documentation required for U.S. tax purposes. [22]

Unlike the U.S., Canada has little experience in the courts dealing with TPMs or valuation. Rather, transfer pricing cases, such as Indalex [23], have been fought on the basis of artificiality or avoidance. However, preliminary court documents have been filed on a transfer pricing case (Smithkline) that will deal with the responsibility of a particular transfer price.

Under the current Canadian Income Tax Act, a person is liable to a penalty to a maximum of $2500 for failure to file or for late filing the T-106 information return. Where Revenue Canada has served a demand for filling the T-106 and the taxpayer has not complied within 90 days, an additional penalty of $1000 per month applies to a maximum of $24000.

Draft legislation released on March 5, 1996, increased the penalties related to the T-106 for returns due after April 29, 1997. The penalty for failure to file the T-106 has been increased to $500 per month to a maximum of 24 months ($12000). Where Revenue Canada has served a demand to file the T-106, within a specified period, and the taxpayer has not complied, the penalty continues to be $1000 per month with a maximum of $24000.

The draft legislation proposes an additional penalty of $24000 per T-106 in circumstances amounting to gross negligence, where the taxpayer has made or participated in, assented to or acquiesced in making a false statement, or omitting information.

Subsection 163(2) and 239(1) deal with circumstances where false statements or omissions of information lead to an understatement of Canadian taxes, and consequently, penalty that range from 50 to 200 % of the tax under payment may apply. There is little, if any, experience in the application of these penalties to transfer pricing matters.

Basis for Determining Non-arm's Length Prices

- Canada should continue to apply the transactional methods endorsed by the OECD when evaluating inter-company transfer pricing used between related parties. [24]
- The general and flexible "reasonable in the circumstances" arm's length criterion of section 69 of the income Tax Act does not require amendment.

Revenue Canada has acknowledged its general acceptance of the OECD guidelines and revisions to Information Circular 87-2 to confirm this acceptance are anticipated. The OECD guidelines agree with the transactional-based approach of the Income Tax Act. Revenue Canada should continue to endorse and follow the OECD guidelines as they appear to achieve the balance needed between protecting the domestic tax base without creating double taxation.

It is recognized as a fundamental principle of Canadian Taxation that members of a related domestic or international group must be taxed on the basis as though they deal at arm's length with each other. However, common ownership allows group members to act with a common objective; such as objective is rarely found in true arm's length transactions. Nonetheless, most MNCs do attempt to take into account various factors when setting inter-company transfer prices and with the encouragement of tax authorities, to use reasonable pricing methods. [25]

Consequently, the OECD states that "tax administrations are encouraged to take into account the taxpayer's commercial judgement about the application of the arm's-length principle in their examination practices and to undertake their analysis of transfer pricing from that perspective. [26]

Nonetheless, as recommended below, Canada should enact documentation standards and penalty provisions targeted at transfer pricing abuses:

Administrative Policies and Guidelines

- Information Circular IC 87-2 should be updated and reissued as soon as possible. It should be more comprehensive in scope and should contain more extensive examples. As well, the Circular should be more specific in identifying the administrative approaches applied by Revenue Canada in evaluating the TPM used by taxpayers.
- Customs and Goods and Services Tax (GST) principles should be more consistent with the Income Tax approach to resolving Transfer pricing disputes.
- An executive interchange program should be initiated between the department and the private sector, where appropriate to encourage the sharing of expertise.
- Revenue Canada should provide guidance on how it intends to use T-106 and tax return reporting in its transfer pricing enforcement and review.

As recommended above, the Canadian transfer pricing principle and policies should be based on the principles enunciated in the OECD guidelines. Canada's application of transfer pricing policies is set out in its Information Circular IC 87-2. This circular was based on the 1979 OECD guidelines and is in the process of being updated. If Canada is to continue to follow the OECD guidelines in general, it is important that any exceptions to the Guidelines be known as soon as possible. Accordingly, Revenue Canada should complete its revisions to the Circular and consider announcing any differences between the Guidelines and the revised circular, before it is released.

With integration of Revenue Canada's custom, excise and income tax divisions, more consistency in application of standards is to be expected.

As noted by the OECD, determining appropriate transfer prices is not an exact science – a great degree of judgement must be brought to bear. Revenue Canada, and taxpayers, have benefited in the past from exchanges of personnel. This practice has been followed, for example, in the rulings directorate. Transfer pricing expertise and experience could be another area where such exchanges are appropriate. It is recognized that there are some issues that would have to be overcome before embarking on such a program. Transfer pricing issues, while perhaps not as technically complex as ruling, do involve a significant period of time being spent together and evaluate relevant information. Potentially, more sensitive commercial information must be disclosed in the course of a transfer pricing review, and enterprises would not wish to share this information with a competitor participating in an exchange program, Nonetheless, this is an idea that should be evaluated as a way to make business experience available to Revenue Canada's transfer pricing specialists.

Revenue Canada has compiled information from T-106s submitted by taxpayers. It is using this information to initiate tax program and audits. [27] Revenue Canada should provide general guidance to taxpayers on how this information is to be used. At present, taxpayers do not know how responses to various questions on the T-106 will affect them, or other taxpayers. For example, the SIC codes used for T-106 purposes are somewhat more condensed than the general SIC numbers, and it is often possible to use more than one (or more) of the T-106 codes to describe a taxpayer. At this time taxpayers are uncertain as to the implications of choosing one code over another. It is recommended that Revenue Canada provides more guidance to, and seek suggestions from, taxpayers on the use and completion of this important form.

Examination Practices

- Revenue Canada should continue the specialized training and status of personnel involved in transfer pricing audits. Involvement of these trained specialists should be mandatory in all transfer pricing reviews.
- TSO transfer pricing specialist personnel should include legal and economic support.
- Until TSO personnel gain more experience, proposed transfer pricing reassessments should be referred to the International Tax Directorate in Ottawa to ensure consistency across the country. Taxpayers should be allowed to participate in the referral process.

As noted in the Ernst and Young studies referred to above, Revenue Canada has been very active in auditing international transactions and MNCs. Revenue Canada has increasingly used trained transfer pricing personnel in its audits of MNCs. This is desirable from both Revenue Canada's perspective and that of taxpayers, particularly given the judgement that must be brought to bear in identifying and resolving transfer pricing issues.

As noted above, transfer pricing disputes do not only have domestic implication. From an international perspective, consistency is expected in similar circumstances. Accordingly, it is important that Revenue Canada's application of transfer pricing policies be as consistent as possible. Under Canada's tax treaties, a mechanism is in place for resolving potential double-taxation issues through the competent authority process with the other country (ies). Canada's competent authority personnel have considerable experience in resolving these matters successfully.

Consequently, it is important that those involved in potential transfer pricing adjustments receive the benefit of this experience, before reassessments are first proposed. While a taxpayer may request such assistance, smaller taxpayers are often reluctant to do so because of concerns about the time and money that may be involved. Revenue Canada may be in a better position to initiate such consultations and should do so as a matter of course to ensue national consistency.

Burden of Proof

Taxpayers should be expected to be able to support the reasonability of related-party transfer pricing through contemporaneous documentation. The extent of documentation needed will vary from case to case, but will not likely be as extensive as that required for U.S. tax purposes.

Under Canada's tax system, the burden of proof in tax disputes often lies with the taxpayer. However, in transfer pricing disputes, it appears that Revenue Canada must show that the taxpayer's method was not reasonable in the circumstances. In effect, the burden of proof is shifted. This may not be an inappropriate result, particularly given the potential for double taxation.

Penalties and Compliance Requirements

- Given the need to balance fairness and simplicity against the pressures of detailed information reporting and the penalties applied under other regimes, and given the need to balance flexibility and uncertain rules against inflexibility and very detailed rules, Canada is well served by less specific rules than those followed in the United States.
- Revenue Canada's initiatives in increasing its review of related-party transactions are warranted; and its continuing advocacy of increased use of simultaneous examinations is desirable. Real time audits of transfer pricing transactions should be encouraged.
- Canada should introduce specific penalties for under reporting of income due to transfer pricing manipulation. Such penalties should differentiate between taxpayers who act in reasonable good faith as evidenced by contemporaneous documentation and those who do not.

Compliance with transfer pricing principles and standards concerns all tax authorities. When one or more tax regimes impose penalties to ensure compliance with their system, other tax authorities will be rightly concerned that taxpayers will be motivated to over-comply with that authority's rules [28], Canada faces that very situation – with its largest trading partner, the United States.

It has been suggested that some balance is needed and that Canada should introduce penalties for non-compliance. In designing any penalties, the following principles should be applied. [29]

- "No fault" or automatic penalties should not be applied. Severe penalties, which apply, based on the mere existence of an understatement are inappropriate, particularly when such understatement is due to an error made in good faith.
- The amount of penalty should be significant enough to warrant attention but not unreasonable. A 20% to 30 % penalty may be appropriate where evidence of reasonable good faith is lacking.
- Penalties should be related to the lack of reasonable documentation and to situations where good faith is lacking.

Given that most T 106 filings appear to involve the United States [30], it is relevant to look to the approach used there. Penalties can be avoided in the United States if there is reasonable documentation in accordance with its penalty regulations. As U.S. affiliates of Canadian taxpayers must comply with the U.S. documentation requirements, and as there are differences in the application of the arm's length standard between the U.S. and Canada, it seems appropriate to base the good-faith standard on whether the taxpayer has compiled documentation reflecting Canadian standards. In addition, the availability of Canadian-oriented documentation should enhance the ability of the taxpayer and Revenue Canada to deal with transfer pricing audits on a timely and more cost-effective basis.

Revenue Canada should have the discretion to waive any transfer pricing penalties pursuant to subsection 220(3.1) of the Income tax Act. This discretion would be appropriate, for example, if the tax reassessed by Revenue Canada is subsequently adjusted pursuant to the competent authority procedures of one of Canada's tax treaties.

Advance Pricing Agreement Program

- The APA program is vital to fair and open administration of the tax system and to keep the Canadian system competitive and fair
- The APA program requires additional resources and a "fast-tract" APA or informal APA procedure should be made available for small companies [31]

Competent Authority

- Canadian taxpayers should be kept fully aware of progress of Competent Authority procedures affecting them.

Taxpayers involved in the competent authority process have expressed concern with the amount of time involved in competent authority resolution of matters and with their perceived lack of involvement in the process. As noted by the OECD, the competent authority procedure is not a process of litigation and the taxpayer's participation should be subject to the discretion of the competent authorities. [32] As the procedure is a negotiation between governments, this conclusion is probably appropriate. Nonetheless, in recognition of the frustrations expressed by taxpayers, the Canadian competent authority should endeavor to keep them informed on a timely basis as to be progress of discussions with the other competent authority.

(i) China

In China, foreign investment enterprises (FIEs), a category that includes wholly owned enterprises and joint ventures, are coming in for increased scrutiny. Currently, there are over 150,000 FIEs in operation in China. These FIEs play a significant role in the Chinese economy. They employ almost 20 million people and account for almost 60 % of Chinese exports and over 50 % of Chinese imports.

The Chinese government has adopted strategic policy toward FIEs. It has encouraged investment in sectors, which it deems beneficial to the economy, viz. high technology while restricting investment in other sectors, viz. services. The government has also used tax holidays and other incentives to steer investment into regions, sectors, and activities that it deems helpful. While, the government has been generally pragmatic and pro-business, it has taken an increasingly hard line towards FIEs who may be abusing these privileges. Transfer pricing is one such area of abuse. In some cases, the FIE may be forced to "buy high and sell low" which results in a loss for the FIE. Meanwhile, the U.S. parent benefits by being able to extract a dividend from the FIE which is disguised as a form of transfer price.

The Chinese Government is convinced that some FIEs are using transfer pricing to avoid paying taxes. For example, many FIEs continue to report losses even as they aggressively expand their operations. The tax authorities believe that such a pattern is an indication that the FIE may be using transfer pricing to engineer losses.

China's hard-line attitude towards transfer pricing is entirely consistent not with third world socialism but with the practices of the most advanced economies. In the United States, over 50 % of the IRS adjustments to multinationals are linked to transfer pricing abuses. China is behind the United States and Japan in aggressively targeting foreign taxpayers but far ahead of other nations in Asia and that it has clear regulations and a specific audit program. In May 1998, the state administration of taxation (SAT) in Beijing issued comprehensive transfer pricing regulations [Guoshufa(1998) No.59]. Next, the Chinese started an intensive training program. At this time there are over 500 local Chinese tax officials who have received transfer pricing training. With so many trained people, an increased level of transfer pricing enforcement is likely.

China has modelled its transfer pricing legislation on OECD principles. Chinese tax authorities consulted with tax experts in the United States and Europe, including inviting PWC to speak to them on transfer pricing in 1997, before drafting Guoshuifa (1998) No.59. China's transfer pricing regulations, consequently, reflect the same arm's length principle that is used in the United States. This principle requires that a parent company treat its associated enterprise on the same basis as it treats an independent enterprise. China also supports the same type of economic methods that are being used in the United States and other OECD countries.

However, it should be noted that transfer pricing enforcement in China is taking a distinctively Chinese character. The Chinese approach is less respectful of economic theories and taxpayer rights. Certain policies acceptable in America are rejected in China. For example, the IRS is urging U.S. companies to charge subsidiaries for the beneficial services provided to them. But China does not allow deductions for management fees. This means that the U.S. management services billed to subsidiaries world-wide may not be deductible in China, unless they have been characterized as some other form of service.

The highlights of China's transfer pricing program, with special attention to those aspects of China's transfer pricing that differ from those in the United States are reviewed here. This information should be useful in communicating in the event of a transfer pricing audit.

The first difference has to do with the nature of the tax authority conducting the transfer pricing audit. In the United States, transfer pricing is enforced by a single federal agency – the IRS. A company with separate legal entities in California and Massachusetts will face only one transfer pricing investigation. That is because the incomes reported by these entities will be consolidated for federal income tax purposes. But China does not allow consolidation of returns. A U.S. multinational with FIEs located in various parts of China will probably be subjected to multiple transfer pricing audits. Moreover, there is no assurance that these authorities will agree. For example, a 5% return for a contract may be acceptable to the tax authority in Xiamen but not to the tax authority in Suzhou or Shenzhen.

The second difference has to do with the types of tax adjustments. In the United States, transfer pricing is seen as a purely federal income tax issue. This may reflect the fact that the United States has no federal sales tax or value added tax (VAT) and customs duties are minimal. In China, however, VAT and customs duties contribute significant revenues. Consequently, Chinese tax authorities will calculate the impact of a transfer pricing violation of such taxes as well. If, for example, it is determined that the Chinese FIE has overpaid its parent for raw materials and been underpaid on final prices, there will be additional VAT of 17% plus enterprise income tax (EIT) of as much as 33%. In addition, the overpayment will be treated as a disguised dividend and a withholding tax imposed. There may also be penalties and surcharges.

The third difference between Chinese and U.S. transfer pricing policies has to do with the process used in benchmarking the earnings for the FIE. Benchmarking involves identifying the earnings of third parties who perform functions that are comparable to the entity in question. The U.S. benchmarking process is more open than the Chinese. The IRS uses commercial databases, also available to the taxpayer, to locate public comparables. In China, tax authorities appear to be developing a database of secret comparables. Out contacts indicate that in Shanghai such a database may be assembled by computerizing the quarterly filing of the financial statements of FIEs. Clearly the possession of such a database gives the authorities a clear advantage over the taxpayer when it comes to economic research.

Another way in, which U.S. and Chinese authorities differ, is with respect to the use of "profit spirit" information. This information is interesting and easy to understand. It shows how the various parties to a transaction share in the profits or losses. But asking for profit spirit information is seen as an unwarranted intrusion. The IRS will request profit split information only as a "last resort". Chinese tax authorities, however, often inquire as to the financial performance of the associated enterprises. For example, the tax authority in Shenzhen requested data on related Hong Kong and Japanese entities. They indicated that a low profit for the contract manufacturing FIE would be unacceptable if the associated enterprises in Hong Kong and Japan were earning significant profits on the resale of these products. This is a very reasonable approach but it is not one that will make the head office happy.

In summary, it is clear that transfer pricing enforcement is evolving rapidly in China. The Chinese approach is tough and practical. While the experience level is lower in China than found in many other countries, there are extensive rules on the books. There is sufficient information at this point to get a genuine sense that China is not going to let taxpayers off easily when it comes to transfer pricing. The Chinese want to make sure that they get a reasonable share of the taxes due to them. Of course, China has to balance this situation with its ongoing need to attract foreign capital. This suggests they will follow the "middle way" which is to enforce transfer pricing regulations with increasing rigor but not apply the severe penalties available in the books except perhaps in the most egregious cases.

FIEs need to keep on top of this issue whether they are fully foreign owned enterprises or in joint venture situations. Naturally, there is a need to inform parent companies in the United States in order to develop a coordinated approach. It is clear that the issue cannot be left alone. Taxpayers should not wait to see if and when the tax authorities investigate. It would be advisable to review inter-company agreements to make sure that they are commercially sound and arm's length in nature. It is also important to ensure that all agreement is in place. It has been our experience that the tax authorities are more likely to challenge transfer pricing and deem taxes in those cases where there are no agreements. If a review indicates that a transfer pricing exposure is significant then it may be advisable to revise the transfer pricing or to develop documentation to support its arm's length nature. In the case of extreme exposure, it may even be advisable to approach the tax authorities and seek an advance ruling, which will secure their pre-approval as to the transfer pricing policies used by the taxpayer.

(j) France

Statutory rules on transfer pricing adopt the arm's length principle for related party transactions. In addition, there are a considerable number of courts cases on issues, which are relevant to transfer pricing, and which aid in the interpretation and application of the legislation. In parallel with increased resources within the tax administration, recent legislative development emphasizes the interest of the French Tax Administration in transfer pricing issues through new rules for documentation and advance Pricing Agreement procedures.

The main statutory rules, which address transfer pricing, are the following:-

(1) Section 57 of the French Tax Code (Code general des impost):

Section 57 was introduced into the French Tax code on 31 May 1933, and since that date has been regularly updated. The most recent update was on 13 April 1996. It can only be applied in relation to cross border transfer pricing issues. Enforcement of Section 57 requires the tax authorities to prove that a dependent relationship existed between the parties involved in the transaction under review and that a transfer of profits occurred. It is now however, necessary to prove dependency when applying S.57 to transfers between entities in France and related entities operating out of tax heavens.

Dependency can either be "legal" or *de facto*". Legal dependency is relatively easy for the tax authorities to prove. It is defined as direct control by a foreign entity of the share capital or voting rights of the French entity under review. It can also mean dependency through indirect control such as through common management. *De facto* control results from the commercial relationship that exists between two or more enterprises. For example, where the prices of goods sold by A are fixed by B, or where A and B use the same trade names or produce the same product, there does not have to be any direct common ownership. However, the fact that a large proportion of two or more companies turnover results from transactions made between them does not necessarily mean that there is de facto dependency. The tax administration of Paris rule on 13 February 1997, that there was a de facto control in the following situation: One French company, in charge of the distribution of books published by a Swiss corporation, was using personnel and equipment provided by a subsidiary of the Swiss entity, had the same management as the Swiss entity and had authority on the choice of books to be distributed.

A transfer of profits can be inferred where, for example, transactions occur at prices higher or lower than prevailing market prices. This includes all types of transactions, including commodities, services, royalties, management services or financing.

(2) The Concept of "acte anormal de gestion" (an abnormal act of management) – the courts decide whether this concept applies by comparing the commercial practices of the company under review with what they judge to be "normal" acts of management.

To invoke the concept of an *acte anormal de gesion* it is necessary to prove that a transfer of profits has actually taken place and that there was a deliberate intention to move profits or losses from one taxpayer to another. It can be applied to both domestic and international transfer prices.

(3) Section L 13 B of the Tax Procedure Code

The Economic and Financial Act, published on 13th April 1996, contains new procedures for transfer pricing examination. The legislation gives the Tax administration a clear right to request information on the tax payers' transfer pricing policy in the course of a tax examination when it has evidence upon which to presume than an indirect transfer of profits abroad has occurred, as defined by section 57 of the French tax code. This new procedure only applies in the course of a normal examination. There is no specific transfer pricing examination, nor any transfer pricing disclosure requirement in France.

Four types of information may be requested under the new procedure:

1. the nature of the inter-company transactions,
2. the method for determining prices for transactions,

3. the activities of the foreign enterprises, companies or joint ventures,
4. the tax treatment of the inter-company transactions.

Until now, the French Tax Administration could request information from taxpayer, but there were no sanctions to encourage compliance with such demands. With the new legislation, in the event of an insufficient response, the Tax Administration will grant the taxpayer an additional 30 days notice. Thereafter, the sanctions imposed on the taxpayer will be two fold:

1. a FF 50,000 fine for each period under audit.
2. the right for the Tax Administration to reassess the taxpayer's profits on the basis of the information at their disposal.

The procedure, however, will remain controversial. The burden of proof of both the dependence links and of the non-arm's length character of the transactions will remain on the Tax Administration.

On July 23, 1998, the French Tax Administration published a regulation commenting on the provisions of Section L 13 B. This regulation specifies in particular that resorting to Section L 13B is neither obligatory nor systematic – it takes place only if the tax inspector has not been provided with sufficient explanations during the tax audit.

Regarding the transfer pricing method used, any method invoked by the enterprise can be considered acceptable, provided that it is justified by the contracts or internal memos describing the method; extracts of the general or analytical accounts; economic analyses, notably on the markets, the functions fulfilled, the risks assumed, and the comparables retained. The French Tax Administration interprets broadly elements required to justify the transfer pricing method.

(4) Section L 188A of the Tax Procedure Code

Section L 188 A provides for an extension of the statute of limitations, and is open to the authorities when they request information from foreign tax administrations before the end of the initial statute of limitations. The new statute of limitation expires either at the end of the year, which follows the year when the information requested is obtained, or failing response at the end of the fifth year which follows the year, which is audited.

For example, if the financial year corresponds to the calendar year, intra-group transactions conducted in 1998 can in principle be investigated with the framework of the authorities investigating a company, unto 31 December 2001. If a request for information is put to a foreign tax authority in December of the year 2001, the transactions may remain open to reassessment for the years 2001-2003.

The extension of the statute of limitation applies if there is a request for information bearing on intra-group transactions or on entities established in countries with favorable tax regimes (CGI s.209 B) but also in cases of requests for information with relevance to the foreign assets, credits, income or activities of a French taxpayer.

(5) 2003 other Regulations

In addition to the legislation specific to transfer pricing described above, the following regulations are also relevant to the issue:

- The terms of various tax treaties,
- Sections of the French tax code which deal with related issues such as transactions with entities in tax heavens, Section 238(a) limits the deductibility in France of commissions and other payments paid to entities located in tax heavens, Section 209(b) allows consolidation in France of profits and losses realised through enterprises located in low-tax regulation,
- A first pure transfer pricing regulation was issued on 4 May 1973 in the form of a "note" (this regulation is the main element of the tax Administration doctrine and in April 1983 the tax authorities finalized and published this commentary on their interpretation with tax heavens),
- A regulation published on 4 March 1986, on competent authority procedure, and
- The tax authorities commentary on legal cases involving transfer pricing, which has been issued over the years in the

form of "directives" (a directive is an indication of how the tax authorities will interpret and apply legal decisions).

In theory, the tax authorities can choose whether to apply s.57 or the concept of "*acte anormal de gestion*" when questioning a transfer pricing policy, in reality, however, this element of choice is likely to be removed by the limitations of each regulation.

Section L 13 B reinforces the French Revenue powers of investigation by imposing new information requirements in case of a tax audit involving transfer pricing. This law facilitates accordingly the application by the Revenue of Section 57.

Section 188 A extends the statute of limitations when the French Revenue requests information from another state under the exchange of information clause of the applicable tax treaty.

France recently announced penalty provisions for non-compliance with the arm's length standard.

(k) Korea

New Korean transfer pricing documentation requirements that went into effect from January 1, 1997, require taxpayers to provide detailed information in tax returns about their inter-company transactions, including profits and losses from the transactions. The documentation requirements apply to taxpayers having total revenues of 10 billion won (approximately $12 million) filing tax returns on or after that date.

Under Notice 1996-40, summarised statements of profit and loss from transactions with overseas related parties, taxpayers who engage in transactions with overseas related parties must submit income statements and balance sheets for the 10 overseas related parties with which they had the most significant amount of annual transactions during the year, regardless of the level of transaction volume with each of the 10 affiliates.

The National Taxation Authority (NTA) pronouncement prescribes the type of additional transfer pricing related documents and information that a resident, domestic company or a Korean branch of a non-resident or foreign corporation must submit when it files its tax return.

Extensive Requirements

The documentation requirements are so extensive, that taxpayers with related party transactions involving inventories are required to provide segmented income statements when the annual amount of related party transactions exceeds 5 billion won.

Moreover, similarly detailed information will have to be provided for the top five overseas-related parties. The term "segmented income statement" is a misnomer since it refers to sales and cost of sales data only and does not include operating expenses. Taxpayers should submit product income statements as well as profit and loss statements on transactions involving:

- The transfer of intangible property, with reports for every transaction involving 1 billion won or more
- The licensing of intangible property, with reports for every transaction involving 100 million won or more
- The transfer of tangible property, with reports for every transaction involving 1 billion won or more
- The renting of tangible property, with reports for every transaction involving 100 million won or more
- Interest or commission transactions, with reports when the average annual balance is 5 billion won or more
- Lending or borrowing, with reports when total lending equals or exceeds 5 billion won

Services

For inter-company transactions involving services, taxpayers are required to provide a statement summarizing the profit and loss from the transactions according to each overseas-related party and type of service. The requirement applies only to the top five overseas-related parties whose annual service transaction volume with the taxpayer is 100 million won or more, according to the provision.

Additional requirements pertain to inter-company financing and the sale or lease of fixed assets.

If the taxpayer performs only sales agent services (Class A trading agent), the amount of transactions will have to be measured by the amount of transactions between the overseas-related party and its buyers in Korea. In the event that the number of inventory items exceeds five, the taxpayer is only required to submit data for the top five inventory items.

The NTA has included a "vague" exception clause since its issuing the notice rather late in 1996. Taxpayers who do not prepare the required income statements in the ordinary course of business may submit other segmented income statements.

The year of financial data submitted for overseas-related parties does not necessarily have to correspond to the year for which the taxpayer is filing its tax return. For example, the taxpayer may submit financial data for 1995 for its offshore-related parties instead of data for 1996 if the financial data for 1995 is the data, which is most currently available. The NTA has acknowledged that this type of detailed data may not be prepared by taxpayers prior to filing their 1996 returns.

Penalties

If a taxpayer decides not to submit the transfer pricing data required by Notice 1996-40, the NTA has said it will request that the taxpayer submit the information at a later date. The taxpayer then has 60 days from the date of request to submit the information requested, according to the provision. Taxpayers may seek a one-time 60-day extension. Failure to provide the information can result in fines on the taxpayers of up to 30 million won (approximately $36,000)

No penalty provisions specifically were set forth in the new rules. However, failure to provide the information could increase the likelihood that the NTA will select the taxpayer for audit.

The disclosure requirements were issued under authority granted by Korea's International Tax Coordination law, which became effective from January 1, 1996. The legislation requires taxpayers to report the transfer pricing method chosen as best fitting their circumstances, allows tax authorities to request pricing data, and establishes an advance pricing approval system.

Noting the extensive changes imposed by Korean tax authorities during 1996, it can be said with certainty that transfer pricing will be one of the most important international tax issues affecting Korean taxpayers engaging in inter-company transactions.

(I) Malaysia

There are to date no known guidelines on transfer pricing in Malaysia. However, there are two sections of the Malaysian Income Tax Act (MITA) which may be invoked by the Inland Revenue Board (IRB) to address any tax avoidance which they view may have arisen from transfer pricing arrangements. The general anti-avoidance provision is Section 140, MITA. Section 141 deals more specifically with arrangements between controlled parties.

A. Section 140

Section 140(1) provides that where the DGIR has reason to believe that any transaction has the direct or indirect effect of (a) altering the incidence of tax, (b) relieving any person from any liability to pay tax, (c) evading or avoiding any duty or liability under the MITA or (d) hindering or preventing the operation of the MITA in any respect, he may, with a view to counter-acting such transactions, disregard or vary such transactions and make adjustments as he thinks fit. His power extends to charging a greater amount of tax than would have been chargeable but for any such adjustments.

Section 140(6) deems that transactions between persons one of whom has control over the other, and between persons both of whom are controlled by some other person, are transactions to which section 140(1) would apply, provided that the DGIR is of the opinion that those transactions had not been made on terms which might fairly be expected to have been made by independent persons dealing at arm's length.

It should be noted that section 140 does not depend on the subjective purpose of the taxpayer, but rather the effect of the transactions objectively viewed, that is, the end accomplished or achieved. If there is commercial justification for the transaction, and where the primary purpose of the transaction is not the avoidance of tax, it may be difficult for the DGIR to invoke Section 140.

B. Section 141

Section 141 is a specific anti-avoidance provision dealing with transactions between Malaysian residents and non-Malaysian persons. Section 141 provides that where the DGIR is of the view that, owing to the close connection between the resident and non-resident and to the substantial control exercised by the non-resident over the resident, the course of business between them is arranged such that the business done by the resident produces either no income or a small income than that which might be expected to arise from that business, the non-resident shall be regarded as having taxable income chargeable in the name of the resident, as if the resident were an agent of the non-resident, has not in fact made but which he might reasonably be expected to have made had he done business on ordinary commercial terms.

Section 141 is directed at transactions, which are arranged such that profits are not taxed in Malaysia. When a true income of the non-resident cannot be readily ascertained, the DGIR may assess the non-resident on the basis of a "fair and reasonable percentage" of the turnover of the business done by the non-resident through or with the resident.

The Assessment Process

The IRB assesses taxpayers based on income tax returns, which have been filed. If the DGIR does not accept the return submitted or does not receive a return, he may proceed to determine the chargeable income of that person "to the best of his judgement". The taxpayer may object to the assessment, in which case settlement discussions will take place, failing which a tax appeal will be heard.

Procedural Rules and Requirements

A. Time Bar

Section 91 of the MITA as it presently reads provides that the DGIR may raise an assessment for a particular year of Assessment or Issue an additional assessment for that Year of Assessment within 12 years of the expiration of that Year of

Assessment if it appears to him that no sufficient assessment has been made on a person chargeable to tax. There is, however, no limitation period if there has been "fraud, wilful default or negligence".

Section 15 of the Finance (No.2) Bill 1997 has amended Section 91 of MITA such that with effect from 1Jan 1999 i.e. from Year of Assessment 2000, the DGIR has to raise assessments within a shorter period of 6 years.

The impact of this change is that from 1 January 1999, instead of being able to raise assessments or additional assessments for income for the basis period of as far back as 1987 (Year of Assessment 1988), the DGIR would only be able to raise assessments for income earned in the basis period of 1993 (Year of Assessment 1994).

In order not to be time-barred by the new rules in Section 91, it is highly likely and expected that before the end of 1998, the DGIR will raise protective (estimated) assessments on taxpayers whom he considers should and would be taxable for the period between 1 January 1987 and 31 December 1998. The practical effect of the protective assessments is that once they are raised, the time-bar in Section 91 ceases to apply. If the taxpayer objects to the assessment, the DGIR would, if he agrees with the taxpayer, merely need to amend the assessment. Amendments of this nature may be made at any time.

B. Power of the Director General to Order Production of Certain Documents

The DGIR has the power to order any person to attend personally before him and produce for examination all documents deemed necessary. He may also order any person to provide in writing such information or particulars, which he deems necessary.

Every person carrying on business in Malaysia has a duty to keep sufficient records to enable the income or loss from the business to be ascertained by the DGIR. If the gross takings from the business exceed RM 150,000(from the sale of goods) or RM 100,000 (from the performance of services), the taxpayer is required to issue serially numbered receipts and retain duplicates. This requirement may be waived by the DGIR.

C. Confidentiality of Information

The IRB is required to maintain the confidentiality of all taxpayer information. Any person who breaches this duty will be guilty of an offence. Confidential Information may, however, be required to be produced in court proceedings for the "prosecution of any offence committed in relation to tax". This exception would not appear significant in the transfer pricing area.

D. Foreign Based Information

The IRB has no power to compel the production of foreign-based information. However, Malaysia's tax treaties generally do provide for the exchange of information and the relevant treaty will govern the powers of the IRB to require the production of such information from that treaty country.

Objections to the Assessment

A. Administrative

The MITA provides an avenue for taxpayers to dispute Notices of Assessment issued by the IRB.

A taxpayer who objects to the Notice of Assessment should lodge his objection in writing with the IRB within 30 days of the date of the service of the Notice of Assessment. Where no objection is made within the required period, the assessment becomes final and conclusive. No objection may be made after this period unless the DGIR is satisfied that there was reasonable cause for the taxpayer's delay.

Notwithstanding the lodgments of a written objection, the tax assessed should still be paid within the statutory period of payment. If it is not paid, penalties will be imposed. The IR may, in special circumstances, hold over on the payment pending an IRB review.

After receipt of the taxpayer's objection, the DGIR would review the assessment. Objections may be settled at this stage between the DGIR and the taxpayer. Where a dispute cannot be resolved, the taxpayer may request for the appeal to be sent to the Special Commissioners.

It is submitted that a Notice of Assessment, once issued, can be withdrawn by the DGIR as he/she is empowered to do so. However, in practice the DGIR is unlikely to exercise this power.

B. Appeal and Judicial Review

There are two ways tax cases can be handled in the courts. The first and most common way is by an appeal to the High Court in relation to a decision of the special Commissioners. The other way is through judicial review by the High Court. In the context of Malaysia, an appeal is more typical than judicial review, which is a rather narrow remedy.

An appeal to the High Court against the decision of the special Commissioners may only be made where the appeal involves a question of law or mixed fact and law. The court may reverse a pure finding of fact by the Special Commissioners for amendment or for further facts to be found.

If either party is dissatisfied with the High Court's decision, an appeal against its decision may be made to the Court of Appeal and then to the Federal Court. There is no right of appeal against the decision of the High Court on a question of fact.

(m) Mexico

The basic transfer pricing rules enacted by the Mexican government is generally consistent with the OECD Guidelines and the rules of U.S. and Mexico's other major trading partners. The reform is a major step in providing Mexico with a tax structure complimentary to and consistent with the trade liberalisation and outward looking economic policies recently implemented by the government.

Changes in Law

The changes made to articles 58, 64-A, and 65 of the Mexican Income Tax Law (MITL) were in part influenced by three principal factors:

- An analysis of the transfer pricing guidelines for Multinational Enterprises and Tax Administrations published by the OECD in 1995 and supplemented in 1996 (the OECD guidelines).

- The actual transfer pricing rules governing major trading partners.
- Mexico's own experience in enforcing transfer pricing principles for companies operating under the country's program for "maquiladoras". These manufacturing and assembly plants have special status that allows them to import component parts duty free and re-export finished products. They may be up to 100% foreign owned.

The 5% Test

Since 1995, these companies have been required either to earn taxable income of at least 5% on the assets employed (including those belonging to non-residents), or to demonstrate that they meet the arm's length standard set forth in the MITL.

If a non-Mexican company meets the 5% test, its tax bill for productive assets owned and used in Mexico relating to the plant will be reduced. This reduction is also available if the foreign interests obtain a favorable resolution from the tax authorities indicating that they have met the Mexican transfer pricing requirements.

Inter-company Transactions

The maquiladora program provided Mexico with valuable information for understanding the development of functional analyses and the application of transfer pricing methods. The Mexican government has rapidly developed an impressive infrastructure for enforcing the arm's length standard, composed of new legislation plus institutional changes designed to implement an effective and practical transfer pricing regime.

A critical element of Mexico's transfer pricing measures is a requirement for all taxpayers with significant inter-company transactions to produce and maintain documentation relating to all inter-company transactions.

They must demonstrate that the transactions are consistent with the amounts that would have resulted from transactions taking place with unrelated parties operating under similar conditions.

Reduced Penalties

Compliance with the documentation requirement entitles the taxpayer to a 50% reduction in penalties in the event that the tax authorities prevail in making a transfer pricing adjustment. Although there are no special penalties for valuation misstatements specific to transfer pricing, the normal penalties for tax assessments still apply.

The normal penalties for valuation misstatements range from 70% to 100% of the taxable amount and from 30% to 40% when the amount of a loss is reduced. Additionally, the amount of the deficiency must be adjusted for inflation and late interest payment must be added, commonly ranging between 2% and 3% per month.

Considering the penalties involved, a company's failure to analyse and document transfer prices in advance in accordance with the law is an undesirable tax and financial position.

(n) New Zealand

Section GD 13(7), prescribes that the arm's length price is determined using one or more of the following methods.

- The comparable Uncontrolled Price(CUP) method
- The resale price method
- The cost plus method
- The profit split method
- Comparable profits method

New Zealand's legislation does not impose a hierarchy for the transfer pricing methods. However, there is effectively a hierarchy in that certain methods may provide a more reliable result than others, depending on the quantity of available data, and a taxpayer's circumstances.

There is however, no requirement for taxpayers to test pricing methods down a hierarchy (either inferred or explicit) to determine an appropriate method. For example, if it appears fairly clear that CUP will not exist for a particular good or service, taxpayer are neither expected nor required to conduct an exhaustive search for comparables to demonstrate that the CUP method cannot reliably be applied before considering the use of an alternative method.

The availability of data is likely to be very important in taxpayer's choice of method. New Zealand is a small market, and thus means reliable comparables may be very difficult for taxpayers to locate.

Inland Revenue acknowledges this concern, and this is reflected in the guidelines approach to the use of foreign entities as tested parties and analysis prepared for foreign jurisdictions. In addition, Section GD 13(7)(d) contemplates the use of profit split method, which is less dependent on comparables than the other pricing methods.

Conclusion

A distinguishing feature of transfer pricing policies, procedures and enforcement is that these matters could be viewed in isolation but must be viewed in a broad international context. As noted by OECD, "In the case of tax administration, specific problems arise at both policy and practical levels. At the policy level, countries need to reconcile their legitimate right to tax a taxpayer based upon income and expenses that can reasonably be considered to arise within their territory with the need to avoid the taxation of the same item by more than one tax jurisdiction. Such double or multiple taxation can create an impediment of cross-border transactions in goods or services and the movement of capital. At a practical level, a country's determination of income and expense may be impeded by difficulties in obtaining pertinent data located outside its own jurisdictions. [33]

In certain countries, including Canada, taxpayers may approach tax authorities to seek advance approval of a transfer pricing method or methods. Such procedures are available on a unilateral, bilateral or multilateral basis. The procedures for applying for an APA in Canada are set out in Revenue Canada's Information Circular 94.4. The general experience has been that it takes companies as long to document their TPMs as it does for the revenue authorities to evaluate the APA submission. Currently,

Revenue Canada is testing a "fast track" APA procedure for taxpayers with relatively low transaction volumes.

Some have suggested that Canadian transfer pricing rules should be made more specific and translated into legislation. As noted previously and pending the outcome of the Smithkline case, there have been no cases dealing with transfer pricing as the sole matter. Accordingly, it is not known whether the current tax legislation has sufficient teeth to deal with transfer pricing abuses. In the meantime other jurisdictions, most notably the United States have set out detailed tax rules and procedures.

It is suggested that, while detailed legislation may be attractive from a purely domestic perspective, it may not allow for the degree of judgement and flexibility required in an international context. Accordingly, a system that sets out a general standard, that is, transactional arm's length pricing method and comprehensive guidelines for applying the standard, such as the OECD Guidelines, should be preferred, particularly for a country that imports capital. It is suggested that the present provisions of section 69 of the Income Tax Act are sufficient for this purpose.

Taxpayers are increasingly using non-traditional resources in dealing with sophisticated transfer pricing issues. For example, the U.S. regulations generally result in an economist or process engineer being used to complete an evaluation functions performed by the related parties. Canada auditors will likely require more direct access to these specialists when dealing with transfer pricing issues, and plans should be made to meet these needs and to provide the necessary resources.

Transfer pricing disputes can be quite complex and expensive as the time and effort needed to develop a document can be considerable. [34] Interpretation of transfer pricing principles can be quite subjective. It is therefore not surprising that the evaluation of a particular transfer pricing policy will vary from taxpayer to taxpayer and between individual Canada auditors, as such decisions will reflect not only the relevant facts and circumstances but also the experiences of the individuals involved. Accordingly, it is important the consultations be open and that as much experience as is available be brought to bear.

However, taxpayers must assume some responsibility for supporting their transfer pricing policies, even in the absence of a pending tax audit or challenge. As noted in the 1996 Ernst and Young study, few respondents intended to prepare documentation for non-U.S. purposes. From a domestic perspective, particularly given the continuing controversy about the CPM, this is probably not acceptable. In the absence of voluntary documentation, it seems appropriate for Canada to introduce documentation requirements of its own.

It is recommended that this documentation be restricted to sufficient information to support the reasonability of the method chosen by the taxpayer for transfer pricing purposes. Unlike the U.S. system, which requires the best method be selected, choice of a reasonable price should not require that all other methods be evaluated. [35]

It is suggested that the following documentation be required:

- An outline of the business and inter-company relationships
- Details of inter-company transactions
- The transfer pricing method(s) chosen
- Relevant supporting information and analysis, including comparables
- Special conditions, e.g. market penetration strategies, affecting inter-company pricing
- A functional analysis.

In the case of companies dealing with related parties in the United States, most of this information should be available from the documentation required under the U.S. transfer pricing legislation, resulting in relatively little incremental cost in developing supporting documentation for Canadian Tax purposes.

The APA program is a welcome development and provides a reasonable means to reduce transfer pricing exposure. The APA program is still in its early stages and, with the exception of modified procedures for smaller, fast track APAs, should be continued in its present form until more cases have been considered and resolved.

These comments summarise the difficulties facing jurisdictions that wish to protect their tax base while not unduly encubalance flow of goods, services and capital.

Appendix

International Transfer Pricing at a Glance

Country	Arm's length standard	Follows OECD guidelines	Explicit TP Rules	Formal TP Document ation	TP Penalties	Advance rulings provided
			Effective Date (mm/yy)			
Argentina	•	•	12/98	12/98		•
Australia	•	•	07/83	09/95	07/83	•
Austria	•	•				
Belgium	•	•	07/99	07/99		•
Brazil			01/97			

Canada	•	•		01/99*	01/99*	•
Chile	•		01/98			
China	•	•	07/91			•
Colombia						
Czech Republic	•	•	01/93			
Denmark	•	•	01/99	01/99		
Finland	•	•	01/31			•
France	•	•	09/85	04/96	04/96	•
Germany	•	•	02/83			•
Hungary	•	•	01/92			
India	•					

Ireland, Republic of	•	•				
Italy	•	•	12/86			
Japan	•	•	04/86			•
Kazakhstan	•		01/99			
Korea	•	•	01/96	01/96	01/96	•
Luxembourg	•	•				
Malaysia	•	•				
Mexico	•	•	01/94	01/97	01/97	•
Netherlands	•	•				•
New Zealand	•	•	04/96	04/96	04/97	•

Norway	•	•				
Peru	•					
Poland	•	•	11/97			
Portugal	•	•				
Russia	•		01/99		01/99	
Singapore	•	•				
Slovak Republic	•	•	01/98	01/98	01/98	
Spain	•	•	01/96			•
Sweden	•	•				
Switzerland	•	•				•
Turkey					01/99	•

United Kingdom	•	•	07/99	07/99	07/99	•
United States	•	•	01/28	01/94	01/94	•
Venezuela	•	•	10/99*	10/99*	10/99*	•
Vietnam						

* Effective dates apply to taxation years beginning after 1998 for Canada and October 1999 for Venezuela.

** References only.

Notes

1. Estimated in the early 1990 and by the Organization for Economic Corporation and Development (OECD).
2. See for example, Article IX of the Convention on Income Taxes 1980 (as amended) between Canada-United States of America wherein it is provided that an arm's length standard is to apply between related parties.
3. OECD, supra, Chapter 1. The accepted standards based on transactional methods and are: comparable uncontrolled price (CUP), comparable uncontrolled transaction (CUT), resale price minus method (RSM), cost plus, transactional net margin method (TNMM), and profit split method (PSM).
4. Compare, for example, the U.S. Internal Revenue Code requirement of an arm's length result and the Canadian Income Tax Act's standard of an amount that would be reasonable in the circumstances between parties dealing at arm's length. The U.S. standard has let to a "bottom-line approach", that may require post-transaction adjustment, whereas Canada takes at a transaction-by transaction approach.
5. There have been other surveys carried out by other parties, for example, a survey by Charles River and Associated in the United States. Such survey results have been fairly consistent with those of the Ernst and Young surveys described in this paper.
6. Transfer Pricing: Risk Reduction and Advance Pricing Agreements, Ernst and Young, 1995.
7. In this 1995 survey, 25 companies were surveyed in each of Australia, Canada, France, Germany, the Netherlands and the U.K.; 50 U.S. and 10 Japanese companies were surveyed.
8. The Canadian, German, Dutch and U.K. authorities commented on the survey results or on the APA process.
9. Over 90% of Canadian MNC respondents have faced queries from Revenue Canada, 48% of the Canadian respondents were involved in Revenue Canada reviews of their transfer pricing at the time of the survey.
10. 46% of larger MNCs said they considered the possibility of review by revenue authorities to a great extent when setting a TPM; only 26% of smaller companies would do so to a great extent. Only 17% of companies that had not been subjected to tax authority review of

their TPM considered the possibility of an investigation when setting a TPM.

11. 7% of respondents tailored their TPM to U.S. rules. Other respondents cited Germany, Canada and Japan.
12. This concern is reinforced by the 1996 survey of documentation practices, infra. On the other hand, a number of companies, concerned about the exposure to penalties, have applied for bilateral APAs.
13. Many Revenue Canada auditors state that these are "easy marks" for some type of adjustment; companies often get lazy in backing up these charges.
14. However, slightly less than half of Canadian respondents thought their company would use an APA.
15. 1995 Transfer Pricing Documentation Survey, The Year in Review, Ernst and Young, 1996.
16. Under this method, the profit performance of a related party is compared with the profit performance of arm's-length companies performing similar functions. Detailed procedures are set out in the Regulations to the U.S. Internal Revenue Code.
17. See, for example, joint release 94-3 issued by Revenue Canada and the Department of Finance on January 7, 1995.
18. OECD, supra, para 3.1. The OECD guidelines suggest that the TNMM can be used as a last resort as a profit-based method the CPM is dismissed as a method unless it corresponds with the arm's length principle. Some U.S. authors have suggested that the TNMM is equivalent to CPM; this position is not generally accepted (see, for example, a speech presented by Carole Gouin of Revenue Canada at the June 6-7, 1996 meeting of the Canadian and U.S. branches of the International Fiscal Association, in Montreal).
19. These documents are to be prepared contemporaneously with the filing of the Corporation's U.S. tax return and must be provided to the IRS within 30 days of being requested.
20. IRS forms 5471 and 5472 are used to report this information.
21. Revenue Canada referred to the ATO and IRS reporting forms when developing its T-106 form.
22. It is unclear at this time whether the information can be obtained through the IRS under the Treaty in the event the taxpayer refuses to provide the information to Revenue Canada directly.
23. 88 DTC 6053(FCA).

24. Revenue Canada endeavours to apply three preferred transactional methods, CUP, resale minus and cost plus. When it is not possible to do so, or if Revenue Canada considers it more appropriate, other methods including profit splits, may be used. Each of these approaches is approved by the OECD.
25. At paragraph 1.2 the OECD states: "Tax administrations should not automatically assume that associated enterprises have sought to manipulate their profits. The consideration of transfer pricing should not be confused with the consideration of problems of tax fraud or tax avoidance even though transfer pricing policies may be used for such purposes".
26. OECD, supra, P-5.
27. See note 2, supra.
28. The OECD makes a similar observation at Para 4.26 of its guidelines (supra).
29. The OECD guidelines comment that the member states concur that sizable no-fault penalties are unduly harsh in good-faith situations and should not be applied where taxpayers have made a reasonable effort to comply with the arm's length standard, OECD, supra, para 4.28.
30. See note 2.
31. Currently Revenue Canada has accepted two smaller, fast track APAs for consideration.
32. OECD, supra para 4.58.
33. OECD, supra, p.P-1, para 4.
34. See comments on the 1996 Ernst and Young documentation survey, supra.
35. Revenue Canada suggests that all methods need to be considered. For example, the APA program requires that a taxpayer explain why a particular method is not considered appropriate for the transaction(s).

6

Transfer Pricing and Taxation in India

Transfer pricing policies and practices have to work within a certain professional framework. They have to satisfy the legal and tax requirement as also the ethical norms. This is important as several loopholes are there for tax avoidance and evasion. In the hands of MNCs, transfer pricing is one of the few handles to subvert the interest of the host country, and thereby, to promote their own limited profit objectives. To this end, the rich industrialised countries have made relevant legislative provisions as discussed in the preceding chapter. The measures taken in this connection in India, forms the subject matter of this chapter. About one third of the chapter is devoted to tax considerations, another one third concerns with accounting treatment and disclosure of such inter-corporate transactions and the rest analyses the implications of new provisions.

Early Provisions

It is curious enough that for a long time there has been no specific law on the matter in India. This country has a long history of foreign MNCs and transnational companies (TNCs) operating right from the days of the East India Company. That apart, the erstwhile managing agents were virtually the multinational functioning in the Indian corporate sector. It is a big question mark as to how the companies like Hindustan Lever Ltd., Glaxo Ltd. And Colgate Palmolive Ltd., etc. were being monitored and controlled with regard to their transfers from parent organization to the Indian subsidiaries and affiliates and *vice versa.* Under Section 92 of the I.T. Act, which was introduced in 1961 and remains unchanged since then, the assessing officer (AO) is empowered to levy tax on profits which he believes an Indian party should have reasonably made in its dealing with a foreign party. While a transfer pricing legislation generally provides detailed guidance in the form of methods to determine arm's length pricing, this provision provides only a very rough guide in rule 11 of the Income Tax rules. This rule discusses how arm's length profit is to be determined. These methods can never achieve the basic aim of transfer pricing which is allocation of income to its true economic source, due to inherent distortions. Both the specific methods referred to in rule 11 read with rule 10, i.e. percentage of turnover method and global formulatory method are specifically rejected by the OECD as not reflecting the arm's length principle.

This principle can be invoked by the AO only where a business is carried on between an Indian party and a foreign party. For instance, if an Indian software company were to transfer its intellectual property right to an off shore company, it can be argued that he Indian company should not be hit by this provision. Also, this provision empowers the AO to adjust the income of the Indian party only and not of the foreign party. Even if the foreign party makes no actual profits, the AO is yet empowered by this section to attribute a profit to the Indian party normally made in that line of business. For example, in the case of Mazgaon Doc *Vs* CIT (34 ITR 368) decided by the apex court, and Indian subsidiary was engaged in the business of repairing ships for its foreign parent, was in turn, engaged in the business of plying ships. The Indian subsidiary repaired ships of its foreign parent company without charging profits. The fact that he dealings were such as to yield no profit to the foreign parent was immaterial and the AO was yet empowered to attribute a profit to the Indian subsidiary normally made in the business of ship repairing.

Transfer pricing adjustments by the AO can be carried out even where export profits are tax sheltered. For instance, an Indian company X, which sells services or goods to its U.S. parent Y, which, in turn, packages these services/goods and sells them to customer reflects a profit of Rs. 50 million and claims the same as tax free because of an available tax holiday under section 10A of the I.T. Act.

This is shown in Table 6.1. The assessing officer believes that from its line of business, X should have earned a profit of Rs. 70 million, were it operating on an arm's length basis with Y. Invoking this power under section 91, he holds this amount to be the correct profit of X. Now, taking things a bit further, it is possible that the officer may impute a higher turnover, say Rs. 120 million because of imputing higher profits. The export turnover would however remain the same at Rs. 100 million, as it would be the amount that would be received in India. This will automatically lead to some profits being taxed. This is because the exempt profits depend on the ratio of export turnover to total turnover. With the total turnover being increased and export turnover remaining constant, the proportion of profit exempt (70 x 100/120) would be less than 100%.

Table 6.1

Transfer Pricing Adjustments

(in million Rupees)

Y	X		Assessing Officer
	Export Sales	100	120
	Less Cost	50	50
	Profit	50	70
U.S.A.			
India	Less: Tax holiday (u/s 10 A)	50	58
	Taxable Income	-NIL-	12

Assessing Officer Empowered to Disallow Expenditure not at Arm's Length

Section 40A (2) empowers the AO to disallow any expenditure, which in his opinion, is in excess of arm's length and is paid to specified related parties. There are no guidelines on what is an acceptable arm's length price. NO power is given to AO to make a corresponding adjustment in the hands of the specified related parties, resulting in double taxation. Also, if the taxpayer sells goods or services at a discount and charges only a lower net price, he does not incur any 'expenditure' and therefore no disallowance under this provision can be made. As far as inter-corporate transactions are concerned, this provision defines related parties in terms of direct equity holding of 20% or more, it does not use criteria such as indirect, through subsidiaries, holding or management control to determine whether parties are related. These criteria, and more, are today commonly applied in developed transfer pricing regulations to determine whether parties are related. In fact, even the Indian tax treaties as well as accounting standard 18 on related party disclosures use these criteria to determine whether parties are related. As a result of these inadequacies, there can be certain situations, which will not fall within the purview of this provision. For example, A and B are two Indian companies having a common U.S. parent – A and B, do not have holding in each other, Purchase made by A from B would not be affected by this section.

Deemed Accrual of Income

Under section 9 of the I.T. Act, income arising directly or indirectly to a non-resident, from any business connection in India shall be deemed to be income arising in India. This provision, however, provides only a very rough guide in rule 10 of the Income Tax rules.

Units Availing Tax Holiday

There are provisions, which grant tax holiday to units fulfilling certain criteria, such as section 10A, in the case of export, section 80 IA, in case of units engaged in infrastructure development. These provisions, however, seek to discharge the tendency amongst taxpayers for using transfer pricing as a mode to maximise the profits eligible for the tax holidays. This is done by empowering the AO to review prices and profits and consider only arm's length prices/profits for granting tax holidays. However, no detailed guidelines are provided and hence, the complex issue of transfer pricing are unable to be addressed

Onus of Proof and Penalties

Under the Indian Income Tax Law; the onus of proof is on the tax officer. But, if the AO Shows, *prima-facie,* that the transfer pricing policy of a taxpayer is inconsistent with the arm's length principle, the burden of proof with respect to showing the correctness of the transfer pricing policy would shift to the taxpayer. There is no specific transfer pricing penalty regime where concealment of taxable income is suspected, penalties ranging from 100% to 300% of the tax sought to be evaded may be levied. Further more, interest may also be levied for non-payment of advance tax on the adjusted profit, currently at the rate of 18% per annum.

Indian Tax Treaties

With a view to imparting objectivity and fairness to Indian units of overseas multinationals over the years, India has entered into certain treaties. The purpose of such agreements has been to ensure that the profit of related parties should be determined on arm's length basis and various tax concessions would only be granted of this income. Notably, unlike the Indian I.T. Act, the concept of related parties in the treaties covers even indirect interest, management control, etc. The treaties merely enable the AO to apply the transfer pricing provisions contained in the I.T. Act and they do not enlarge the scope of these provisions. Thus, there is a potential for unfair advantage to a state which has a comparatively aggressive approach to transfer pricing in its domestic tax law. The treaties tend to provide for a grievance platform for aggrieved taxpayer in the form of mutual agreement procedures. Some treaties also provide relief in the form of consequential transfer pricing adjustment following article 9(2) of the OECD Model.

The expert group, a committee appointed to recommend possible legislative changes in the I.T. Act relating to transfer pricing has submitted its recommendation to the Central Board of Direct Taxes on January 1, 2001. The expert group's recommendation included introduction of transfer pricing legislation in line with practices prevailing internationally.

Exchange Control Implications

Income Tax implication apart, transfer pricing could have implications under exchange control regulations (FEMA) as well. In export, to ensure that there is no under-invoicing of merchandise export, an exporter needs to file a declaration before the customs department, showing the full export value of the goods, and receive the foreign exchange corresponding to such values into India. Customs authorities certify the value declared by the exporter. In the case of imports, to guard against over-invoicing on imports, the Reserve Bank of India has directed authorised dealers to exercise due precautions while releasing foreign exchange for importers.

Accounting and Reporting

Financial statements of a company are required to depict a true and fair view of the state of affairs and operating performance of the company. The auditors are required to discuss, in their report, whether or not, the financial statements portray a true and fair view of the state of affairs of the company. Related party transaction could have a significant bearing on the financial position of a company. Currently, auditors of public companies have to include an opinion on whether such transactions are at arm's length. For this purpose, auditors generally apply broad level tests. As transfer pricing legislations in India mature, the auditors would be in a position to take a close look at transfer pricing issues.

Recently, the Institute of Chartered Accountants of India (ICAI) has introduced two standards, namely

1. Segment Reporting (Accounting Standard 17)
2. Related Party disclosures (Accounting Standard 18)

1. Segment Reporting (Accounting Standard 17)

This standard comes into effect in respect of accounting periods commencing on or after 1.4.2001 and is mandatory in nature, from that date, in respect of the following:

(i) Enterprises whose equity or debt securities are listed on a recognised stock exchange in India, and enterprises that are in the process of issuing equity or debt securities that will be listed on a recognised stock exchange in India as evidenced by the board of directors' resolution in this regard.

(ii) All other commercial, industrial and business reporting enterprises, whose turnover for the accounting period exceeds Rs. 50 crores.

In measuring and reporting segment revenue from transactions with other segments; inter-segment transfer should be measured on the basis that the enterprise actually used to price those transfers. The basis of pricing inter-segment transfers and any change therein should be disclosed in the financial statements. Changes in accounting policies adopted for segments reporting that have a material effect on segment information should be disclosed. Such disclosure should include a description of the nature of the change, and the financial effect of the change if it is reasonably determinable. An enterprise should indicate the types of products and services included in each reported business segment and indicate the composition of each reported geographical segment, both primary and secondary, if not otherwise disclosed in the financial statements. This would provide comprehensive data in respect of various activities carried on by an entity. This would facilitate transfer-pricing analysis both by the taxpayer and tax collector.

2. Related Party Disclosures (Accounting Standard 18)

Accounting Standard 18, which becomes mandatory in respect of accounting periods commencing on or after 1.4.2001, stipulates reporting related party relationships and transactions between a reporting enterprise and its related parties.

According to the standard, "parties are considered to be related if at any time during the reporting period one party has the ability to control the other party or exercise significant influence over the other party in making financial and / or operating decisions.

The standard deals with "related party relationship described in (a) to (e) below:

(a) Enterprises that directly, or indirectly through one or more intermediaries, control, or are controlled by, or are under common control with, the reporting enterprise, this includes holding companies, subsidiaries and fellow subsidiaries;

(b) Associates and joint ventures of the reporting enterprise and the investing party or venturer in respect of which the reporting enterprise is an associate or a joint venture.

(c) Individuals owning, directly or indirectly, an interest in the voting power of the reporting enterprise that gives them control or significant influence over the enterprise and relatives of such individual;

(d) Key management personnel and relatives of such personnel; and

(e) Enterprises over which any person described in © and (d) is able to exercise significant influence. This includes enterprises owned by directors or major shareholders of the reporting enterprise and enterprises that have a member of key management in common with the reporting enterprise.

The Standard further clarifies, "the following are deemed not to be related parties":

(a) Two companies simply because they have a director in common, notwithstanding paragraph (d) or (e) above, unless the director is able to affect the policies of both companies in their mutual dealings;

(b) A single customer, supplier, franchiser, distributor or general agent with whom an enterprise transacts a significant volume of business merely by virtue of the resulting economic dependence; and

(c) The parties listed below, in the course of their normal dealing with an enterprise by virtue only of those dealings, although they may circumscribe the freedom of action of the enterprise or participate in its decision-making process:

(i) providers of finance

(ii) trade unions

(iii) public utilities

(iv) government departments and government agencies including government sponsored bodies.

It would appear that the coverage of related parties in the Standard is quite comprehensive. It is likely to cover all situations, which are proposed to be covered under the definition of "associated enterprises" as per Finance Bill, 2001, under section 92 of the Income Tax Act as well as the "inter-connected undertakings" under MRTP Act. Further the disclosure required under the Standard does not confine itself to domestic or international transactions. Hence, for every legal entity, it is required to disclose related party relationships and transactions with its related parties, in respect of accounting periods commencing on or after 1.4.2001.

New Legislations

Since early nineties with the opening up of the economy, more and more multinationals have set up business base in India. With this trend, problems related to the transfer pricing has become more significant. To resolve these problems and to ensure that India gets its fair share of taxes with the globalization of the Indian economy, the Central Board of Direct Taxes (CBDT) set up a committee under the chairmanship of Shri Raj Narain, to formulate the transfer pricing regulations in India.

Based on the recommendations of the Raj Narain Committee, the Finance Act 2001, made for reaching amendments to the

Income-Tax Act, 1961 by replacing the existing section 92 with detailed provisions contained in section 92 of 92F.

The new provisions, effective April 1 2001, deal with computation of income arising from international transactions between associated enterprises. These provisions are a very important step taken by the country in the field of anti-avoidance. Further, the term "Associated Enterprises" has been defined wide enough to rope within its ambit organisations which have associations of any type. The terms 'transactions' and 'international transactions' have also been defined very widely to include virtually dealings of every type.

In May 2001, the CBDT circulated draft rules relating to the new regulations, seeking public comments. The rules have since been finalised. For effective administration, the CBDT has also set up an exclusive cell for dealing with foreign tax assessments, including transfer pricing. For this purpose, the CBDT has created a new post viz., Director General, International Tax(DG), which is equivalent to a rank of the Chief Commissioner. One of the important functions of the DG is to seek clarifications and liaise with tax authorities of other countries.

The earlier section 92 of the I.T. Act has been completely substituted by sections 92 to 92F of the I.T. Act to provide for a framework to regulate transfer pricing. The new regulations are in line with the OECD guidelines. This section now provides that income arising from international transactions, between associated enterprises, would be computed having regard to the arm's length price. As such, section 92 acts as a computation section.

The language of section 92(1) raises fundamental issue as to whether it applies to case of pure expenditure. To interpret the section narrowly would be unwarranted as it is a settled legal position that the term "income" includes 'expenditure'.

It is further provided in section 92(2) that the allowance for any expenses or interest in respect of such a transaction would also be determined having regard to arm's length price. This provision may lead to unintended result, as the deductibility for expenses or interest on an arm's length price is not prefixed by a condition that the transaction should be an international transaction. The possible rationale interpretation and reconciliation of section 92 would read sub-section (1) and sub-section (2) as harmonious, and applicable to income and expenditure arising from international transactions.

Most of the jurisdictions provide for what is commonly known as "Advance Pricing Arrangements" (APAs) and "Safe Harbour Rules" in the transfer pricing regulations. However, these do not find place in the new regulations.

Important Definitions

International Transaction and Transaction

"International transaction" has been defined as a transaction between two or more associated enterprises, one or both of whom are non-residents.

The definition also covers transactions between head office and branch. The transactions intended to be covered are purchase, sale or lease of tangible or intangible property, provision of services, lending and borrowing of money, cost sharing and any other transaction which have a bearing on the profits, income, losses of assets of an enterprise. As such, virtually every conceivable transaction is proposed to be roped in for scrutiny.

"Transaction" means any arrangement, understanding or action in concert, whether formal or in writing and whether enforceable or not. As such, all understandings between parties would be regarded as transactions.

Associated Enterprises

The term "associated enterprises" is defined to include any enterprise, which participates directly or indirectly in the management or control of capital of another enterprise. It includes enterprises under common management, control and ownership. The term is deemed to include enterprises covered by a variety of circumstances, including enterprises which are inter dependent on each other by virtue of borrowings, guarantees, licensing of trade marks, purchases, sales or whether enterprises have "mutual interest' as may be prescribed by the CBDT. It may be important to note that under the guidelines issued by the OCED, mere existence of participation in capital not accompanied by participation in management or control does not result in enterprise being regarded as an associate.

Arm's length price has been defined to be the price which independent parties charge under uncontrolled conditions.

Methods to Determine Arm's Length

Section 92 C prescribed the following methods as being most appropriate in determining the arm's length price:

- **Comparable Uncontrolled Price Method**

The comparable uncontrolled price (CUP) method compares the price charged for property or services transferred in a controlled transaction to the price charged for property or services transferred in a comparable uncontrolled transaction. Under the OECD guidelines, the CUP method has priority over alternative methods, if comparable uncontrolled transactions exist, because the CUP method is the most direct and reliable method available.

- **Resale Price Method**

The resale price method (RPM) compensates a reseller of goods for costs incurred and provides an appropriate profit for functions performed, tangible and intangible assets employed, and risks borne. The resale price margin is derived from the resale price margin of the same reseller on items purchased and sold in comparable uncontrolled transaction, or from the resale price margin of an unrelated party engaged in comparable uncontrolled transactions. The RPM is generally applicable to marketing or distribution operations.

- **Cost Plus Method**

Under the cost plus method (CPM), an arm's length price is determined by applying an appropriate mark-up on costs incurred. The underlying rationale is that a 'cost plus' mark-up provides an appropriate reward for the functions performed, assets employed, and risks borne by the taxpayer. Costs t be taken into account include direct and indirect costs.

This method generally relies upon margins computed after direct and indirect costs of production, rather than net margins, which allow for selling, general and administrative expenses. The cost plus mark up is derived from the mark up on costs of the same supplier in comparable uncontrolled transactions or from the mark-up on costs of an unrelated party in comparable uncontrolled transactions.

There are 'other methods' or transactional profit methods', which rely on information either on the level of profits made by one party to a comparable arm's length transaction or on how the overall profits made by both parties to such a transaction would be divided between them. These methods often known as 'fourth' methods include the rate of return, profit split transactional net margin and the Berry ratio.

- **Profit Split Method**

The profit split method (PSM) determines the division of profits that independent enterprises would expect to realize under circumstance similar to transaction under review. The profit split method calculates the profit, either total or residual, from the controlled transactions and splits those profits based on the contribution of each entity and is therefore consistent with what would have occurred at arm's length.

The contribution of each entity is determined by performing a functional analysis and valued, if possible, by reference to reliable external market data. In performing a profit split analysis on a residual basis, combined profits are divided into two states.

In one stage, profit is allocated to each participant to provide a basic return for functions performed, ordinarily a market return based on the returns of independent entities.

In stage two, the residual profit or loss is allocated based on facts and circumstances that indicate how the residual would be divided between independent enterprises. It focuses on intangible property contributed, relative bargaining positions, and reference to external market date.

- **Transactional Net Margin Method**

The transactional net margin method (TNMM) examines the net profit from controlled transactions as a percentage of a base viz. costs, sales, and assets. Ideally, the net margin should be established by reference to net margins earned by the same taxpayer in comparable uncontrolled transactions.

If that is not possible, the TNMM refers to comparable transactions between independent entities. Comparability between controlled and uncontrolled transactions is established through a functional analysis.

Quantitative adjustments must be made to account for material differences between the controlled and uncontrolled transactions. Use of an arm's length range, rather than appoint, can further reduce the effect of difference between the controlled and uncontrolled transactions.

The TNMM considers only the profits of the controlled entity that are attributable to the transactions under review. The application of the TNMM on a company-wide basis is inappropriate if the company engages in a variety of different controlled transactions that cannot be compared on an aggregate basis with those of an uncontrolled comparable company.

- **Such Other Method as may be Prescribed by the CBDT**

In case more than one price is determined by applying the most appropriate method, the arm's length price shall e taken as to be the arithmetical mean of such prices. This is one more departure from international practice where a price range is the accepted standard.

Where more than one method is found to be "most appropriate", the method which yields result which is more approximate to the third method would be regarded as the most appropriate method. This provision in the rules is a bit strange and possibly not warranted. Rather than provide for such intellectual exercises, it would be simpler to let an assessee chose any method where two methods are "equally appropriate".

Powers of Assessing Officer

Based on the material and information available, the AO in the course of assessment proceedings, can determine the arm's length price where price is not in accordance with the proposed provisions of prescribed information is not maintained or data used for computing such price is not reliable or correct or prescribed information is not furnished.

The burden of proof would be on the AO for determining the arm's length price if the price determined by the assessee is not considered by him to be at arm's length.

Penalty Provisions

The new provisions provide for multiple penalties. Penalties have been proposed for:

- Misstatement of valuation, which will be deemed to conceal income (100%-300% of the additional tax)
- Non-maintenance/filing of prescribed documents (2% of the transaction value);
- Non furnishing of the Accountants' Report(Rs. 1 lac)

There is no exemption in case where the price is ultimately found to be "arm's length price".

However, it has been provided that no penalty will be levied in case where there is a reasonable cause for default, except in the case of income concealment. It would indeed be welcome if a clarification is issued that penalties would not be levied for technical default where no concealment is detected. This would do away with situations where penalty is imposed only for technical breaches like non-maintenance of documents as considered appropriate by an Assessing officer, even if the pricing is found to be arm's length.

No deduction would be allowed under section 10A/10B or under Chapter VIA of the I.T. Act in respect of any enhanced income resulting from such re-determination. It seems to suggest that the enhanced income would not be regarded as derived from prescribed activities.

Draft Rules

The draft rules issued by CBDT can be divided into the following three parts:

- Part I, dealing with the manner in which the prescribed methods will be applied in determining the arm's length price.
- Part II, dealing with the information and documents to be maintained by any person entering into an international transaction
- Part III, dealing with furnishing of Accountants' Report in a prescribed form.

The practical issues arising out of the Rules are discussed below under the relevant headings.

Determination of the Most Appropriate Method

The draft rules provide for the manner and factors to be considered in a applying the most appropriate method. The key factors prescribed are class of transactions, availability of data, degree of comparability with unrelated transaction, possibility of making adjustments for difference, etc.

Practically there would be various other factors, which could impact the arm's length price. These could be in the form of Government restrictions, market penetration strategy, etc. This difficulty can be addressed by defining factors "inclusively" rather than "exclusively".

The choice of method under the new Regulations has been rightly left to the assessee. However, the draft rules provide that the transaction-based method (CUP, CPM and RPM) will be preferred over the profit-based methods (PSM and TNNM). Incidentally, U.S.A prefers to adopt the best method route to arrive at the arm's length price. Interestingly, Brazil adopts a method that yields lowest taxable income.

Further, the requirement as per the draft rules for comparing two methods, which could be most appropriate with a third method so as to arrive a "the most appropriate method", could be onerous. Also, the applicability of RPM method has been restricted to goods; it needs to be extended to services, etc.

In case of applying RPM, the same is required to be based on net profit margin, which is contrary to global practice based on gross profit basis.

In case of CPM, the adjustment contemplated relates to profit margin and not costs. Further, there is no adjustment margin prescribed in relation to the final price.

Section 92D, requires every person entering into an international transaction to maintain prescribed information/documents in respect thereof, for a prescribed period and furnish information/documents in the course of I.T. proceedings. Further, such person is required to obtain and furnish a report from an accountant in a prescribed form within a prescribed period.

The information and documentation to be maintained has been prescribed under the drat rules. The proposed list includes the following information/documents, which would be onerous and in some cases practically not possible to comply with:

- List of all associated enterprises, including those with whom no international transaction have been entered into,
- Third Party agreements,
- Accounts of associated enterprises and tax treatment likely to be accorded in the country of residence.

The above assumes importance because non-maintenance of prescribed information / documentation could lead to levy of penalty @ 2% of the transaction value.

It needs to be recognised that internationally information and documentation is required to be maintained keeping in mind the costs and administrative difficulties faced by the assessee and after considering the magnitude of the transaction.

The issue regarding confidentiality of the information furnished to the AO needs to be addressed seriously since the current provisions of the I.T. Act (section 138) are not stringent. Unless the section is significantly amended to ensure confidentiality, it could lead to unintended results. This issue assumes significant importance in light of provision for levy of separate penalty for non-furnishing of information/documents called for.

Also, it would add to administrative burden to maintain prescribed information / documentation where there is enough evidence to show arm's length price. Except to a very limited extent, the internationally prevailing threshold limits for maintaining information is also absent.

Furnishing of Accounts' Report

The new regulations require every person who has entered into international transaction with an associated enterprise to furnish an accountants' report within the due date of filing of the return of income. The accountants' report prescribed under the draft rules is to be obtained and furnished to the AO irrespective of the value of the international transaction. In other words, there is no threshold limit for obtaining and furnishing the report. It will be a great relief to the assessee if the CBDT before finalising the rules prescribe a threshold limit as above.

It is interesting to note that there is no corresponding amendment made to section 139 of the I.T. Act to provide that the accountants' report need to be submitted along with the return of income.

Some Issues

Arithmetical Mean vs. Range of Price

As per Indian transfer pricing regulations, in case more than one price is determined as arm's length price under the most appropriate method, the arithmetical mean of such prices should be considered the arm's length price.

However, since transfer pricing is not an exact science and it may be practically possible that two comparable uncontrolled transactions take place at two different prices, such rigid requirement for a particular price may not be fair on the taxpayers.

Further, OECD supports the concept of an arm's length range of prices for the purpose of transfer pricing.

Multiple Year Data – No Provision

The newly introduced transfer pricing regulations specifies that any adjustments, by the tax officer, to the income or expense of the taxpayer would not result in a corresponding adjustment to the expense or income of the associated enterprise of the taxpayer.

Confidentiality

Confidential data like trade secrets, pricing policies etc. that is submitted to tax authorities must be kept confidential. The law as it currently stands does not provide for regulations to ensure that such information is not disclosed to third parties in general and competitors in particular.

OECD's Suggestion for Minor Modification to the Draft Rules

In view of certain peculiar features of the Indian transfer pricing regulations, OECD has made the following suggestions to modify the Indian transfer pricing regulations, essentially to bring it in line with international practice:

- Difference in the prices estimated by the tax authorities and the taxpayer should be acceptable, if the difference falls within the range of 10% to 15%. This suggestion is in line with the range concept, which forms a part of OECD's transfer pricing guidelines. As per the said guidelines, the differences in estimated prices may be caused by the fact that the application of the arm's length principle may produce only an approximation of conditions established between independent enterprises.
- A provision be included in the Indian transfer pricing regulations to allow the taxpayer to base the arm's length price determination on data pertaining to earlier years. This would allow a comparison of the company's transaction prices for the current year and earlier years. It would also help in determining whether the independent enterprises engaged in comparable transactions were affected by comparable economic conditions.
- The transfer pricing regulations should allow the taxpayer to use methods not specified in the transfer pricing rules, so long as

those methods satisfy the arm's length principle in accordance with the guidelines.

International Comparison

A comparative analysis of international transfer pricing regulations discussed in the preceding chapter vis-à-vis Indian Regulations is given in Table 6.2 and 6.3.

Conclusion

From the foregoing it is obvious that transfer-pricing policy never works in the vacuum. It is affected by legal, tax and accounting guidelines of the host country. In turn, the transfer pricing also affects these aspects. A transfer pricing is a continuous process, and has to keep itself abreast of the developments in the environment. Indian laws have been alive to this issue, powerful as it is. This is a clear-cum response to fresh challenges posed by overseas multinationals. This also signifies globalisation and maturing of the Indian economy. Although this new insertion has been widely welcomed, the precise impact will be judged in a year or two.

Table –6.2

International Comparison

Parameters	**Acceptable Methods**	**Priority of Methods**	**Advance Pricing Arrangements**
OECD	CUP,RPM,CPM, PSM, TNMM	Transaction based methods preferred to profit based methods	Option available to tax payer
India	CUP,RPM,CPM, PSM, TNMM	Transaction based methods preferred to profit based methods	No statutory provision
U.S.A.	CUP, RPM, CPM, Comparable Profit split method, Residual Split method	Best method	Option available to tax payer
U.K.	CUP, RPM, CPM, TNMM, PSM	Most reasonable method. Transaction based methods preferred to profit based methods	Option available to tax payer
Japan	CUP,RPM,CPM, PSM, other similar method	Transaction based methods Preferred to profit based methods	Option available to tax payer
Germany	CUP,RPM, CPM, PSM	Transaction based methods Preferred to profit based methods	No statutory provision. Taxpayer can apply to authorities

Table – 6.3

International Comparison

Parameters	Penalties	Documentation and Disclosure	Time limit for Adjustments
OECD	10 % - 200% of additional tax. Bonafide -Partial relief	Tax return should contain information that would allow authorities to comply with requirement	To be determined under local laws
India	100% - 300% of additional tax. Non-maintenance / filing of documents – 2 % of transaction value. Non furnishing of report – Rs. 1 Lac	Business overview, ownership structure, commercial agreements, method selected, authentic documentation etc.	2 years from the end of assessment year
U.S.A	20%-40% of additional tax. No penalty – if methods reasonably applied	Business overview, method selected, alternative method, rejected comparable etc.	3 years from due date or actual date of filing return – whichever is later
UK	Up to 100% of additional tax. Bonafide -Partial relief	Assessee to maintain appropriate record to demonstrate reasonable pricing	6 years from end of the accounting year
Japan	10% - 40% penalty on incremental tax	No statutory provisions Details like method selected, Comparable etc. called for	6 years from due date of filing return
Germany	No penalty	No statutory provisions. Details like method selected, Comparables etc called for	4 years from due date of filing return

Appendix

Laws Relating to Transfer Pricing at a Glance

Sec.	Effective Date of Amendment	Nature of Amendment	Effect of Amendment
1	2	3	4
92	1-4-2002	Section 92 to 92F shall be substituted for Section 92.	Section 92, relating to income from transactions with non-residents, how computed in certain cases, shall be substituted by new sections 92, 92A, 92B, 92C, 92D, 92E and 92F relating to computation of income from international transactions having regard to the arm's length price, meaning of associated enterprise, meaning of international transaction, computation of arm's length price, maintenance of information and documents by persons entering into international transactions, furnishing of a report from an accountant by persons entering into international transaction and definitions of certain

			expressions occurring in the new sections. Section 92 shall be substituted to provide that any income arising from an international transaction shall be computed having regard to arm's length price. Sections 92A and 92B provide meanings of the expressions "associated enterprise" and "international transactions" with reference to which the income is to be computed under section 92. Section 92C provides for computation of arm's length price. The section provides that he arm's length price in relating to an international transaction shall be determined by (a) comparable uncontrolled price method (b) resale price method; or (c) cost plus method, or (d) profit split method; or (e) transactional net margin method; or (f) any other

			method which may be prescribed by the Central board of Direct Taxes. One of these methods shall be the most appropriate method which shall be applied for computation of arm's length price in the manner as may be specified by CBDT in this behalf. In a case where more than one price can be determined by the most appropriate method, in such a case the arm's length price shall be the arithmetical mean of such two or more prices. The new section further provides that where during the course of any proceeding for the assessment of income the Assessing Officer is, on the basis of material or information or document in his possession, of the opinion that the price charged in the international transaction has not been determined in accordance with sub-section (1) and (2) or information and

			documents re3lating to international transaction have not been kept and maintained by the assessee in accordance with the provisions contained in sub-section (1) of section 92D, and the rules made in this behalf or the information or data used in computation of arm's length price is not reliable or correct or the assesses has failed to furnish, within the specified time, any information or document which he was required to furnish by a notice issued under sub section (3) of section 92D, the Assessing Officer may proceed to determine, after giving an opportunity of being heard to the assessee, the arm's length price in relation to the said transaction in accordance with sub-sections (1) and (2) of this section, on the basis of such material or information or documents available with him.

			Section 92D provides that every person who has entered into an international transaction shall keep and maintain such information and documents as may be specified by rules made by the CBDT. The CBDT may also specify by the rules the period for which the information and documents are required to be retained. During the course of any proceedings under the Act, an Assessing Officer or Commissioner (Appeals) may require any person who has entered into an international transaction to furnish any of the information and documents specified under the rules within a period of thirty days from the date of receipt of a note issued in this regard and such period may be extended by a further period not exceeding thirty days. Section 92E provides

			that every person who has entered into an international transaction during a previous year shall obtain a report of an accountant and furnish such report on or before the specified date in the prescribed form and manner. Section 92F defines the expressions 'accountant', arm's length price, 'enterprise', 'specified date' and 'transaction' used in the proposed new sections 92, 92A, 92B, 92C, 92D and 92E.
271(1)	1-4-2002	Explanation shall be inserted	Section 92 is substituted by sections 92, 92A, 92C, 92D and 92E and 92F arising to computation of income arising from an international transaction. Explanation 7 shall be inserted in sub-section(1) of Section 271 to provide that where in the case of an assessee who has entered into an international transaction defined in section 92B,

			any amount is added or disallowed in computing the total income under sub-section(4) of section 92C, the, the amount so added or disallowed shall be deemed to represent income in respect of which particulars have been concealed or inaccurate particulars have been furnished. However, the provisions of this Explanation shall not apply where the assessee proves to the satisfaction of the Assessing Officer (Appeals) that the price charged or paid in such transaction has been determined in accordance with the section 92C in good faith and with due diligence.
271AA	1-04-2002	Shall be inserted	Section 271AA relating to penalty for failure to keep and maintain information and documents, in respect of each international transaction, shall be inserted. Section 271AA provides

			that if any person who has entered into an international transaction as defined in section 92B fails to keep and maintain any such information and documents as required by sub-section (2) of section 92D, the Assessing Officer or Commissioner (Appeals) may direct that such person shall pay, by way of penalty, a sum equal to two % of the value of the international transaction entered into by such person.
271BA	1-4-2001	Shall be inserted	Section 271BA, relating to penalty for failure to furnish a report from an accountant under section 92E, shall be inserted. Section 271BA provides that if any person fails to furnish a report from an accountant as required by section 92E, the AO may direct that such person shall pay by way of penalty, a sum of one hundred thousand rupees.
271G	1-4-2002	Shall be	Section 271G relating to

		inserted	penalty for failure to furnish certain information or document, under section 92D, shall be inserted. Section 271G provides that if any person who has entered into an international transaction fails to furnish any such information or document under sub-section (3) of section 92D, the AO or the Commissioner (Appeals) may direct that such person shall pay, by way of penalty, a sum equal to 2% of the value of the international transaction, for each such failure.
273B	1-4-2001	Certain words shall be inserted	The existing provision of section 273B provides that no penalty shall be imposable on the person or the assessee, as the case may be, for any failure referred to in certain sections specified in the said section, if he proves that there was reasonable cause for such failure.

			Section 273B shall be amended to provide that no penalty shall be imposable on the person or the assessee, as the case may be, for any failure referred to in section 271AA, 271BA, 271G, if he proves that there was reasonable cause for such failure. The amendment is of consequential nature.

7

Corporate Cases in Transfer Pricing

The discussion so far has been largely of the principles and practices with regard to transfer pricing. It is difficult to claim originality in the material. In a topic like this, which centres on the figures, it is the case studies which give a feeling of real life. We have selected three companies in the pharma sector, which are either conglomerates or Indian multinationals. These are Dabur India Ltd., JK Drugs and Pharmaceuticals Ltd., and Ranbaxy Laboratories Ltd. These are star performers in the Indian corporate sector and are poised to unscale heights.

On the basis of the information collected, the case studies have been prepared. The facts and figures obviously have been camouflaged. This chapter emphasises the significance of pharma industry in India and the rest discusses the case studies.

Pharmaceutical Industry in India

The pharmaceutical industry in India is in the front rank of India's science based industries with wide ranging capabilities in the complex field of drug manufacture and technology. It holds a leadership position in the third world, in terms of technology, quality and range of medicines manufactured. From simple headache pills to sophisticated antibiotics and complex biotechnology derived products, almost every type of medicine is now made in India. Not only India produces pharmaceutical formulations but over 350 active pharmaceutical ingredients are manufactured from basic stage. Ancillary industry is also fully developed and full range of pharmaceutical manufacturing equipment is locally produced.

The organised sector of the pharmaceutical industry has played a key role in promoting and sustaining development in this vital field. International companies associated with this sector have stimulated, assisted and spearheaded this dynamic development in the past fifty four years and helped to put India on the pharmaceutical map of the world.

The Indian Pharmaceutical Industry today is in the front rank of India's science-based industries with wide ranging capabilities in the complex field of drug manufacture and technology. A highly organized sector, the Indian Pharma Industry is estimated to be worth $ 4.5 billion, growing at about 8 to 9 percent annually. It ranks very high in the third world, in terms of technology, quality and range of medicines manufactured. From simple headache pills to sophisticated antibiotics and complex cardiac compounds, almost every type of medicine is now made indigenously.

The value of the pharmaceutical market in India was U.S. $ 6.0 billion in 2004. It grew by 6.4% over 2003. Although India accounts for 16% of the world population, the sales of pharmaceuticals is just 1.8% of the global sales in terms of value and 8% in terms of volume. Globally, it ranks 4th in volume and 14th in value terms

The pharmaceutical industry in India has quality producers and many units are approved by regulatory authorities in U.S.A. and U.K. It has a pool of personnel with high managerial and technical competence as also skilled workforce. Its track record of development, particularly in the area of improved cost-beneficial chemical synthesis for various drug molecules is excellent. It provides a wide variety of bulk drugs and exports U.S. $700 million worth of bulk drugs. The Indian Pharmaceutical sector is highly fragmented with more than 20,000 registered units. It has expanded drastically in the last two decades. The leading 250 pharmaceutical companies control 70% of the market with market leader holding nearly 7% of the market share. It is an extremely fragmented market with severe price competition and government price control.

The Indian market has some unique advantages. India has a 54 year old thriving democracy. It has an educated work force and English is business language. It has a solid legal framework and strong financial markets. Over 9000 companies are publicly listed.

Professional services are easily available. There is already an established international industry and business community. It has a good network of world-class educational institutions and established strengths in information technology. The country is now committed to a free market economy and globalisation. Above all, it has about 100 million middle class market, which is continuously growing.

For the first time in many years the international pharmaceutical industry is finding great opportunities in India. The process of consolidation which has become a generalised phenomenon in the world pharmaceutical industry has started taking place in India. The Pharmaceutical Industry, with its rich scientific talents and research capabilities, with intellectual property protection regime on the anvil, is well set to mark its place as a sunrise industry.

The prime mover in influencing the operating environment of the pharmaceutical industry is the Government's drug policy. Currently, the drug policy of 1986, as modified and rationalised in 1994, is prevailing. The Drugs (Prices Control) Order 1995 (DPCO 95) outlines the classification of price controlled/ decontrolled products and methods of price fixation and revision. The National Pharmaceutical Pricing Authority (NPPA) monitors the prices by fixing and revising prices of drugs. The 347 price controlled drugs under the Drugs (Prices Control) Order 1979 were brought down to 143 in the Drugs (Prices Control) Order 1987. Under DPCO-95, there are 74 bulk drugs and their formulations under price control covering around 40% of the total pharma market. The policy-makers have recognised the need for giving incentives for Research and Development (R&D) in the Indian Pharmaceutical Industry and believe that import liberalisation process will require the industry to improve its competitiveness. The Government is, therefore, planning to bring down the span of price control to around 25% of the total market in India.

The lack of world-class Intellectual Property Rights (IPRs) is identified as a deterrent to attracting foreign direct investment and accelerating R&D in the Indian pharmaceutical industry. The general approach to pharmaceutical patent production has changed recently in India and even the domestic industry is reconciled to the benefits of a strong IPR regime.

The Government has introduced a Patents (Second Amendment) Bill ("The Bill") to amend further the Patents Act 1970, the first amendment of which grants Exclusive Marketing Rights. The Bill has been referred to a Joint Committee of both the Houses of Parliament. The Committee is evaluating various comments and suggestions by interest groups and will submit a report to Parliament, who will then consider the Bill to enable the Government to incorporate suitable amendments in the existing Patents Act, 1970. The new IPR regime will act as an incentive to induce and develop a strong innovative culture in India for developing newer and improved medicines.

Case Studies

1. Dabur India Ltd.

Established in 1884, Dabur India Ltd. is one of the oldest health and personal care companies in the country. It also enjoys the distinction of being the biggest Indian FMCG Company and is all set to become a true Indian multinational. The company's revenue today exceeds Rs. 8 billion. It plans to achieve a turnover of Rs.20 billion by the year 2003. It is today a multi-location enterprise employing a task force of over 5,000 people and having 11 manufacturing plants in India, Nepal and Egypt. It has a shareholder fraternity of 34,000. The company also has a manufacturing license in the Middle East. In India, Baddi (Himachal Pradesh) has been making rapid progress with new manufacturing facilities being commissioned at a satisfactory pace.

Distribution Network

After production, distribution is another major strength of the company. A transnational distribution network of more than

5,500 distributors is serviced through 21 sales offices. This network ensures availability of its products in more than 13,00,000 retail outlets in India. The company has sales and marketing offices in Dubai, London, New York and Moscow. Its manufacturing facility for injectibles has withstood stringent quality measures of MCC of South Africa and OGYI of Hungary. The anticancer drugs of the company are registered in countries like Russia, Kenya, Peru, Brazil, Sri Lanka, Philippines, etc. Its products are currently being exported to over 50 countries across the globe.

Product Portfolio

Dabur has a product portfolio, which has eight brands, having market share of over 65%. These products are positioned at varied socio-economic cross-sections, thus providing products for literally every household. In the last couple of years Dabur has added cosmetic goods to its range. The major areas of company business activity today comprise the following:

(a) Personal Care Products

This is the largest business unit in terms of sales turnover. The major products lines are:

- Hair Care - Amla Hair Oil, Vatika Hair Oil and Shampoo, Anmol Coconut.
- Oral Care - Red Tooth Powder, Binaca Range.
- Foods - Honey, Sharbat-e-Azam, Gulabari, Kewra Water.

(b) Health Care Products

This business unit has some of the best-known brands of Dabur. This is the oldest division, as Pudin Hara was one of the three original formulations marketed by Dr. S.K. Burman. Now, here major product lines are:

- Herbal Tonics - Chayawanprash, Restog.
- Digestives - Pudin Hara, Hajmola Tab, Hajmola Candy, Hingoli.
- Mother and Child Care - Janam Ghutti, Lal Tail and Gripe Water

(c) Ayurvedic Specialties

Traditional ayurvedic medicines sold ethically through ayurvedic practitioners are promoted by this division. This division has a range of over 300 classical and proprietary ayurvedic medicines in its portfolio. These products are divided in 16 categories. Major product lines are:

- Asav-Arishtas
- Ras Rasayana
- Medicated oils
- Churans
- Proprietary medicine

(d) Food and Cosmetics

This is the youngest business unit of Dabur. It handles a range of ethnic Indian food products and a range of 33-skin care and hair care products sold under the brand name, Samara. The principle product lines here are:

- Real fruit juices
- Homemade ethnic cooking pastes and sauces
- Capsico chili sauces
- Nutra Salt low sodium salt
- Samara beauty therapies

(e) New Drugs

On the basis of its own R&D, the company has succeeded in introducing two new drugs in the market. These are Intaxel (Paclitaxel), and Daxotel (Docetaxel) both derived from Asian Yew trees. Dabur is only the second company in the world to manufacture these formulations. Dabur Research Foundation (DRF) developed the unique eco-friendly process for extraction of these drugs from leaves of the tree.

(f) Confectionaries and Foods

Dabur's joint venture with Agrolimen of Spain is manufacturing bubblegum under the brand name Boomer and candies by the name of Bonker Excelcia Foods Pvt. Ltd. Dabur joint venture with Osem of Israel is marketing cream filled crisps under the brand name Creamwich. Some new products are also ready to be introduced in the market by this company. Bongrain of France, one of world's biggest cheese companies, is partner with Dabur for another joint venture set up for manufacturing and sale of specialty cheese and dairy products.

Transfer Pricing

The company has two divisions namely:-

(i) Manufacturing

(ii) Marketing

The company is a decentralised organisation having the following features:

- it has two divisions or segments;
- each division having autonomy regarding its segment;
- segment managers make decision within the constraints of the company, overall goals, objectives, plans and policies.

Policy

The Company's core policy is to realise a profit margin of 5% on the total cost. Thus, the transfer price of the manufacturing division to the sales division is determined by adding 5% margin on the total cost. Of course estimation is made of the expected inflation. Cost escalation as a result of likely increase in the prices of inputs is given due recognition.

Procedure for Calculation

The procedure for calculation of cost of each product and determining the prices of the transfer to the marketing division is given below:

- Raw material, Packing Material and Excise Duty have been considered on actual basis.
- Calculation of conversion cost is based upon following procedure:-
  - First Cost Centerwise expenses taken from Cost Centerwise report
  - Grouping of Cost centers based on their nature, Production related, FOH related, Utility related
  - Process-wise total cost calculated

- Calculation of Standard man-hour product-wise
- Calculation of Process-wise Cost/Standard Man-hour
- Calculation of Product wise/Process-wise conversion cost i.e. Cost per man-hour x Product-wise standard man-hour

Observations

It is observed that Dabur India Ltd. has been following the rule of thumb transfer pricing policy. It is an across the board an addition of 5% the total absorption cost. Such a policy might have helped the company in the shelter market, which the company has had so far. Once Indian competitors and foreign players enter the field, this approach may not survive. Another drawback of this policy is that it is far from market forces. Once a rational policy is adopted, the company's turnover may increase many folds. A sound policy is based on segmented approach.

2. J.K. Drugs and Pharmaceuticals Ltd.

The company is a division of J.K. Industries Ltd. The turnover of this division was Rs. 109.72 crores for the year ended March 31, 2000. Sales of formulations increased by 34% compared to previous 12 months. The company also launched some product extensions. During the year, the focus of the formulation division has been to consolidate and grow its existing products. There has been a substantial improvement in the sale of major products like NODD, EXIME, J.K. Fiam and J.K. Clox while cefadrol and oxyfree showed good promise. A number of diabetic camps held across the country have helped position Gilk as a good anti diabetic product. The generic formulation grew well in terms of volume and the company now is among the leading generic formulators in India. Export of formulations has also shown a consistent growth during the period 1999-2000.

The formulation business continues to be the area of focus for the growth of the company. A set of new line extension is being introduced to support the existing branch in the therapeutic segments of gastrointestinal nutrition and non-steroidal anti-inflammatory drugs (NSAID's). In addition, the company has lined up to launch some new generation formulations especially in the NSAID and Anti diabetics segments. The business of intermediates and API's has also started showing sign of improvements as a result of enriched product mix and long term tie up and with international companies. The company is working towards few more long-term ties ups with the international companies. The process of registration of formulation in many more countries is being pursued actively enhance the export formulations business.

Research and Development

Shripati Singhania Research and Development Center (SSRDC) is credited with developing in short time technology for a number of intermediates and API's which have led to a long term tie ups as mentioned earlier. The Center also continues to up grade the existing technologies for APJ's so as to retain their competitiveness. SSRDC has also been able to develop innovative dosage forms for some of the formulation and a few products with new drug delivery systems. The new product will be launched in the ensuing year. The Center has been rigorously pursuing work for registrations in the international markets both for formulation as well as API's.

Human Resource

The company continues to give high importance to growth and motivation of its valuable resource the talented manpower. Regular training programs for employees at all level are organised to meet the ever-growing needs of the business.

Transfer Pricing

The company has three divisions (Process) namely:

1. 7 ADCA (7 Amino Di Chloride Acid)
2. Bulk Drugs
3. Formulation.

Company

7ADCA (Intermediate)	Bulk Drugs	Formulation

The company is a decentralized organisation having the following characteristics:

(i) It has three operating divisions or segments.

(ii) Each division has autonomy regarding its operating segment.

(iii) Segment manager's decisions made within the constraints of the company's overall goals, objectives, plans and policies.

The 7ADCA Division produces Amino di chlorides acid. The basic raw material for this is penciline G. Some other chemical and acids are also added during the first process.

Bulk Drugs Division: In this division the output of 7 ADCA is used as raw material. The finished product of the division is cephalexin. To produce one kg. of cephalexin, 710 gram of 7 ADCA is used as the basic raw material.

The cost of producing one kilogram of Cephalexin in the division is Rs.4150. The market price of cephalexin (the finished product of Bulk drugs division) is Rs. 3850. Forty percent of total product of this division is sold in the market and sixty percent of the product is transferred to the next process namely formulation at market price i.e. Rs.3850 per kg.

Formulation

In this division the output of Bulk Drugs Division, Cephalexin is used as basic raw material. The finished product of this division is cephalexin capsules 500 mg. and capsules 250 mg.

Observations

The Company's transfer pricing policy is to charge market price for the transfer of products from one division to another.

The company is using arm's length price for inter-division transfers. The market price is determined by the market forces i.e. demand and supply of the product and the company is not in a position to influence the market prices. This is fair enough. In two divisions – 7ADCA and bulk drugs part of output is used for captive consumption and part of the product is sold in the market.

3. Ranbaxy Laboratories Limited

Ranbaxy is among the few Indian Companies to recognise the importance of global market place. The company's global market has been broadly classified into four regions. Each region has unique product and market characteristics and the most appropriate organizational structure has been put in place be it a subsidiary, a joint venture or a distribution agreement. Ground level understanding of the dynamics of each market within each region helps them preempt and respond to market conditions with speed and aggression in furtherance of their objectives of becoming a truly global organisation.

The following observations capture the company's performance in each of the region providing insight into each market and the plans towards the achievements of the company's objectives. One of the fundamental strengths of the company has been its capabilities in research and development (R&D). Sustained commitments and serious investments in R&D are beginning to deliver as the company concluded its first major R&D with Bayer AG. The plan and preparedness of this function follow the regional descriptions. The company's committed workforce is keeping well apace of the dynamic changes that information and communication technology are heralding together. The company is well geared to access any information at any place at any time which translates to better service and higher profits.

- **Region –I: India and Middle East**

India and Middle East Region accounts for approximately half of the company's global business turnover. During 1999 the region achieved increases sales of Rs. 8809 million.

India

The Indian pharmaceutical market which contributes over 90% of the regions revenue maintain its dominant position in Indian pharmaceutical market and has been featured as the 4th largest stand alone business (Source ORG- MAT Dec. 1999).

Middle East

Strengthening Runway's presence further seven more products were registered in the UAE market. In Oman 12 new products were registered after a gap of four years. Ranbaxy expanded its market in Sri Lanka with the launch of SimVor.

- **Region –II: Europe, CIS and Africa**

The year was marked with success for the region with sales worth US $ 60 million, by combined sales (including subsidiary companies) recorded a remarkable US $ 74 millions. The major focus areas for the region continued to be UK, Continental Europe, Russia and UK rain belt, Nigeria, France, West Africa Egypt and South Africa.

- **Region –III: Asia Pacific and Latin America**

The Asia- pacific and Latin American markets have been expanding markets, product portfolios. Ranbaxy's performance in this large and diverse market has been very encouraging and the region delivered higher than expected sales and profits.

- **Region – IV: North America**

Maintaining the momentum generated during the last year Ranbaxy Pharmaceutical Inc. (RPI) launched a number of products during the 12 months, significantly expanding its product portfolio, reflecting a 17% growth in its performance.

Transfer Pricing

There are two main divisions:

Manufacturing

Marketing

Manufacturing (Pharma)

Bulk Drugs | Formulation | Research and Development

Production is located in India as well as overseas. The output of bulk drugs divisions is either used for captive consumption or is marketed. Modes of transfer price vary from business to business.

In a vertical integrated company the transfer price can be

1. Variable cost + Some fixed cost (Or)
2. Full cost

In substance transfer price for production division is based on marginal cost to full cost.

- ***Transfer Price for Manufacturing to Marketing:*** A transfer price for manufacturing to marketing is the market price i.e. arm's length price. For formulation a transfer price varies from marginal cost to full cost.
- ***Transfer Price Overseas***: Two segments

1. Export 2. Tax

New Industrial undertakings get tax concessions u/s 80 IA.

- ***Transfer Pricing in Subsidiaries*** Transfer pricing in affiliated companies is determined on the basis of economic value of affiliated companies.
    - Sales
    - Market and Sales
    - Product Development

The economic value of earnings would reside where the risk reside.

- ***Gross Product Sales - Affiliates*** - Retention of Profits
    - It should be arm's length price
    - It should coincide with the economic risk in terms of market conditions.

Observations

The company has two divisions namely manufacturing and marketing. Transfer price for manufacturing to marketing is the market price i.e. arm's length price. Transfer pricing in formulation varies from marginal cost to full cost. The price of the transfer to the affiliated companies is determined on the basis of economic value of such companies. So the company's policy of transfer pricing is different for different divisions.

Conclusion

It is observed that in these case studies, that different companies follow different transfer pricing policies. There is no uniformity.

In the case of first company i.e. Dabur India Ltd., the policy has been full cost plus 5% (profit). This is simple enough but it deviates from arm's length price.

In the case of second company i.e. J.K. Drugs and Pharmaceuticals Ltd. the policy is arm's length price so that company is using market price for internal transfers. This is fair enough.

In the case of the third company, i.e. Ranbaxy Laboratories Ltd, the company is using different transfer pricing for different divisions. Transfer price for manufacturing to marketing is market price. Transfer pricing in formulation varies from marginal cost to full cost and so on. So the company's transfer pricing policy is flexible and foresighted.

8

Issues in Transfer Pricing and Alternatives

Since the economic reforms signaled in 1990-91, there has been a globalisation and maturing of the Indian economy. Each year has seen the entry of new multinationals (MNCs) into the country, and domestic companies growing into the conglomerates by adding products and locations. A large number of MNCs made their presence felt on the Indian shores for the first time. Reverse has also been true; many Indian companies have also set up their operations outside the country. Sheer coincidence, technology and competition have come at the centre stage. These two environmental factors greatly impacted on the organisational structure and culture. In the brave new world, the convergence of information, tele-communications and broadcasting has led the spread of Internet. The web based inter-connectivity has blurred the business borders across the globe, unthinkable a few years ago. The online transactions have further energised the cult of MNCs and conglomerates.

Pharmaceutical Industry in India

The pharma industry in India has been one of the front rank science based industries. It has held a leadership position in the third world in terms of technology, quality, and range of medicines manufactured. Ancillary industry has received enough impetus, and full range of related equipment has been indigenously produced. The organised sector has played a key role in promoting and sustaining development in this vital field. MNCs associated with the sector have stimulated, assisted and spearheaded the dynamic development in the past 54 years, and helped to put India on the pharmaceutical map of the world.

The value of the pharmaceutical market in India was U.S. $ 6.0 billion in 2004. It grew by 6.4% over 2003. Although India accounts for 16% of the world population, the sales of pharmaceuticals is just 1.8% of the global sales in terms of value and 8% in terms of volume. Globally, it ranks 4th in volume and 14th in value terms

For the first time, in many years, the international pharmaceutical industry has found great opportunities in India. The process of consolidation which has become a generalised phenomenon the world over has started taking place in India too. The industry, with its rich scientific intellectual property protection regime on the avail is well poised to take its place in the international arena.

Corporate Practice Relating to Transfer Pricing

The transfer pricing methods used in actual practice have been of three main categories, namely cost-based, market-based, and others. Variation have been there within each category, and occasionally a hybrid form has been used. Cost-based prices were a popular pricing mechanism in circumstances where market price were not feasible, or were otherwise not suitable. In most cases of vertical transfers to successive levels of production or distribution where the transferring unit was viewed as a cost centre, the cost based methods of transfer pricing were applied. Horizontal transfer, to similar levels of production or distribution by captive units was also executed at cost, which might include freight and handling charges. The more centralised firm tended to favour cost based transfer as a basis for control decision making and monitoring performance.

Transfer prices might be based on the market price of the semi-finished products or on the ultimate market price. There has been a general agreement that if competitive market for intermediate product existed, market price would be an ideal option. The reason is that it was determined by parties that are external to the firm and dealt at arm's length with one another. Market price, when used for internal transfers was, therefore, the most objective measure of value employed while charging for the goods or services exchanged. Use of market price was consistent with decentralised profit centres orientation. Profits determined by external market were less subject to internal manipulation and were reasonable measure of performance. They also helped to distinguish between profitable and non-profitable operations. Competitive market price thus stimulated control of costs and encouraged efficiency.

Market prices easily fitted into the notion of arm's length price. Among host governments sensitive to anti-competitive practices, a consensus seemed to be emerging that arm's length pricing was an appropriate norm in computing taxable profits. But a major problem associated with it has been the frequent absence of an intermediate market for the product or service in question. This happened in the case of semi-finished products or specialised components. Modified market price might also be used in the intra-company transfer of products and services. The market price might be reduced to make allowance for reduced efforts in selling and transportation expenses that are often characterised inter-division transfers.

The method would, however, not be very appropriate where transfers were made among subsidiaries situated in two different countries. Owing to distance involved economies on shipping etc. would not be realised. In certain situation, however, it might be necessary to revise the market price upward to take care of hidden costs arising on account of buying division making reasonable delivery demand on the selling division, or on the extra costs incurred to meet more stringent quality standards.

In the other category, negotiated price may be used for intra-company transfers. It is also termed as bargained price. This price is determined by bargaining between sub-units, involved. This approach rests on the assumption that the entities have complete freedom to bargain. In other words, if an agreement were not reached on the transfer price they would be free to sell in the external market. Since it is virtually impossible for a single transfer price to simultaneously meet the criteria of goal congruence, sub-unit autonomy and managerial effort, some companies resort to dual pricing. Under this mechanism, a given transaction is recorded at two prices arrived at by using two different methods.

For the multinational firms, the transfer pricing must accomplish two objectives: performance evaluation and optimum determination of income taxes. Subsidiaries are frequently evaluated on the basis of net income and return on investment. As is the case for any transfer price, the selling subsidiary wants a high transfer price that will raise its net income. The buying subsidiary wants a low transfer price that will provide better margin and increase its net income set by the parent company. Therefore, the use of mandated transfer prices makes the use of returns on investment (ROI and net income suspect. They wee not under the control of divisional manager and no longer served as an indicator of management performance. MNCs have used transfer pricing to shift cost to high tax countries and shift revenues to low tax countries.

U.S. based multinationals have been subject to internal revenue service (IRS) code. Section 482 has given the IRS the authority to re-allocate income and deduction among subsidiaries if it believes that such reallocation will reduce potential tax evasion. Basically, this section requires that sales may be made at 'arm's length'. The transfer price set should match the price to be set if the transfer were made by unrelated parties. The IRS allows three pricing methods that approximate arm's length pricing. In order of preference, there are the comparable uncontrolled price (CUP) method, the resale price method (RPM), and the cost plus method (CPM). The CUP method is essentially a market price – that is the subsidiary purchasing product for resale sets a transfer price equal to the resale prices less gross profit. Percentage of cost plus method is simply the cost based transfer price.

Arm's Length Principle

The Organisation for Economic Cooperation and Development (OECD) has adopted arm's length principle for transfer pricing. There are several reasons why OECD member countries and other countries have adopted the arm's length principle. A major reason is that the arm's length principle provides broad parity of tax treatment for MNCs and independent enterprises. This principle has puts associated and independence enterprises on a more equal footing for tax purposes. It avoids the creation of tax advantages or disadvantages that would otherwise distort the relative competitive position of either type of entity. In so removing these tax considerations from economic decisions, the arm's length principle has also been found to work effectively in the vast majority of cases. For example, there are many cases involving the purchase and sale of commodities and the lending of money where arm's length price may readily found in a comparable transaction undertaken by independent enterprises under comparable circumstances.

General Conclusion

As eluded earlier, the basic aim of this book was to examine the various transfer pricing methods used by conglomerates and multinationals. An obvious reason for the choice was the dramatic increase in the network of subsidiaries opened by multinationals. With this trend, problems relating to transfer pricing have become more significant. The major findings of the study have been summarized as under:

The response to the questionnaire, as expected, showed that, a single transfer price was an illusion. The drug firms in India have used market price for some set of transactions, standard cost for another set, and negotiated price for yet another set. However, the arm's length approach has been the eventual destination. Indian pharma corporates have also found merit in this market related price. It has been found to meet the criteria of goal congruence, autonomy and performance evaluation.

The case studies in the thesis have been related to Ranbaxy Laboratories Ltd., Dabur India Ltd., and JK Drugs and Pharmaceuticals Ltd. The first one is perhaps the Indian flagship multinational with a turnover of Rs.1,745.89 crore in the year 2000. Exports at Rs. 811.19 crore constituted 46.5% of the sales in the USA, the UK, Germany, Poland, China, and the African continent. Within the production division, Ranbaxy makes intra-company transfers at full cost. Transfer from manufacturing to marketing is invariably at the market price. In the affiliated companies, it is determined on the basis of the economic value, which includes sales, market and sales, and product development. So the company's policy of pricing intra-company transfer is different for different units.

Dabur India Ltd., the emerging pharma giant of India has had a phenomenal growth in the last decade or so. Its turnover grew from Rs.706 crore in 1996-97 to Rs.1,166 crore, in 2000-01. It has clubbed its six divisions of personal care products, health care products, ayurvedic specialists, food and cosmetics, new drugs, and confectionaries and food into two broad categories viz., production, and marketing. The company has been more or less, following the rule of thumb transfer pricing policy. It transfers the products from production to marketing at full cost plus 5%. It represents an across the board addition of 5% on total absorption cost. This policy is far from market forces. Once a rational policy is evolved, it will be good for the company. A sound policy has to be based on segmented approach.

JK Drugs and Pharmaceuticals Ltd., the third company selected for the case studies, has achieved a remarkable success in the recent past. For the year 1999-2000, the turnover of the company was Rs.109 crore. Worth noting that, it itself is a division of J.K. Industries, an emerging Indian conglomerate with a turnover of Rs.1,346 crore in the same year. The company has three divisions namely, 7ADCA (intermediate), bulk drugs, and formulation. It adheres to the policy of market price. The company has been using arm's length price for inter-division transfers. It is determined by the market forces, and the company is not in a position to influence the price.

With regard to multinationals, the objective of the transfer pricing is certainly the minimisation of the incidence of corporate and other taxes. Since an MNC operates in different countries, it wishes to so arrange the transfer pricing method that larger profits are sought to be shown in those countries which are tax heavens-the countries with no taxation or minimum of taxation. Other important considerations today are restrictions on profit repatriation, and exchange control. It is an aspect of the government, consciousness to loss of revenue as a result of MNCs effort to minimise overall tax liability.

In most of the cases, it is the arm's length application has fulfilled the objectivity of MNCs. If some individual peculiarities were noticed, suitable modification was affected. Surveys conducted in this connection have re-affirmed its supremacy. Several gaps did exist in the country. There have been no specific legislations regarding transfer pricing. The same hold good for accounting and reporting, presentations. A virtual absence of coordination among the Excise, Income tax and Custom departments was surely observed.

Recent Developments

Sales of goods, transfer or licensing of technology and patent rights, and provision of services are the vehicles for the transfer pricing abuses. Section 92 of the Indian Income Tax Act, which provides for preventing such abuses, is found to be insufficient for the purpose. It empowered the assessing officer (AO) to determine and then include in the taxable income of the resident assessee, the amount of profits which might reasonably be deemed to have been derived from such business transaction, as has been arranged, because of the close connection between the resident and the non-resident, so as to yield no profit or loss than the ordinary profits. That section has now been substituted by newer sections viz., 92, 92A, 92B, 92C, 92D, 92E and 92F. The new provisions became operative with effect from 1.4.2002. Section 92 relates to the computation of income from international transactions having regard to arm's length price. Section 92A defines the expression "associated enterprise", and section 92B, "international transaction". Section 92C prescribes the methods for determination of the arm's length price in relation to an international transaction. Section 92D deals with maintenance, keeping of information and the documents by persons entering into international transactions, and, section 92E, with the requirement of obtaining by them a report from an accountant. Section 92F is a definition clause defining various expressions used in the aforesaid sections. Penalties have been provided for failure to comply with the requirement, of the said fresh provisions. Sections 271AA, 271BA and 271G have been newly inserted for the purpose. A new explanation '7' has been inserted in sub-section(1) of Section 271, which deems assessee having concealed particulars of income or furnished inaccurate particulars in respect of amount added or disallowed on arm's length price having been determined.

Furnishing of Accountant's Report

The new stipulations require every person who has entered into international transaction with an associated enterprise to furnish an accountant's report within the due date of filing of the return of income. The report prescribed under the draft rules is to be obtained and furnished to the AO irrespective of the value of the international transaction. In other words, there is no threshold limit for obtaining and furnishing the report. It will be a great relief to the assessee if the CBDT prescribes a threshold limit for the purpose.

The new provisions, in fact, are based on Articles 9(1) of the OECD / UN Tax Model convention for tax agreements between two countries for the avoidance of double taxation unfortunately in all the Indian double taxation avoidance agreements. That Article allows the tax authority to make adjustment to the reported profits to bring them to what is often described as the arm's length profit. The same principle governs the newly inserted provisions. The provision also provides for the computation of arm's length price. These have been drafted on the guidelines as set out by the OECD in 1995 in Transfer Pricing Guidelines for multinational enterprises and tax administrations.

Introduction of A.S.17 and A.S.18

The Institute of Chartered Accountants of India (ICAI) has issued two accounting standards on segment reporting (A.S.17) and on related party disclosures (A.S.18). Both of them have been operative from accounting period commencing on April, 2001. Accounting standard 17 requires companies to furnish detailed information on each business segment. This would provide comprehensive data in respect of various activities carried in respect of an entity. This would facilitate transfer pricing analysis both by the tax payer and collector. Accounting standard 18 on related party disclosures draws inspiration from International Accounting Standard 24. A disclosure of related party relationship and transactions necessary for understanding of the effect of related party transaction on the financial statement is required. Currently, the auditors are required to comment on the arm's length pricing in transactions with only specific related parties, i.e., the parties in which either directors are interested or are under the same management. A.S.18, however, has a broader definition of related parties and will, therefore, cause a specific disclosure of transactions which are currently not being commented upon. Also, the disclosure would tend to alert an assessing officer to examine whether or not the disclosed related party transactions are at arm's length.

Incorporation of transfer pricing regulations in the Income Tax Act signifies globalisation and maturing of Indian economy. It is, as such, a widely welcome step in the right direction. It is necessary that the administration of the legislation is done fairly and penalties are levied in extreme cases without treating them as revenue generating sources.

Appendices

Appendix 1

Relevant Sections of Income Tax Act

Section 92

Computation of Income from International Transaction having Regard to Arm's Length Price

92. (1) Any income arising from an international transaction shall be computed having regard to the arm's length price.

(2) In computing income under sub-section (1), the allowance for any expense or interest shall also be determined having regard to the arm's length price.

(3) Wherein an international transaction, two or more associated enterprises enter into a mutual agreement or arrangement for the allocation or apportionment of, or any contribution to, any cost of expense incurred or to be incurred in connection with a benefit, service or facility provided or to be provided to any one or more of such enterprises, the cost or expense allocated or apportioned to, or as the case may be, contributed by, any such enterprise shall be determined having regard to the arm's length price of such benefit, service or facility, as the case may be.

Section 92A

Meaning of Associated Enterprise

92A (1)For the purposes of this section and sections 92, 92B, 92C, 92D, 92E and 92F, "associated enterprise", in relation to another enterprise, means an enterprise-

a) which participates, directly or indirectly, or through one or more intermediaries, in the management or control or capital of the other enterprise; or

b) in respect of which one or more persons who participate, directly or indirectly, or though one or more intermediaries, in its management or control or capital, are the same persons who participate, directly or indirectly, or through one or more intermediaries, in the management or control or capital of the other enterprise.

(2) Two enterprises shall be deemed to be associated enterprises if, at any time during the previous year: –

(a) one enterprise holds, directly or indirectly, shares carrying not less than twenty-six per cent of the voting power in the other enterprise; or
(b) any person or enterprise holds, directly or indirectly, shares carrying not less than twenty-six percent of the voting power in each of such enterprises; or
(c) a loan advanced by one enterprise to the other enterprise constitutes not less than fifty-one per cent of the book value of the total assets of the other enterprises; or
(d) one enterprise guarantees not less than ten per cent of the total borrowings of the other enterprise; or
(e) more than half of the board of directors or members of the governing board, or one or more executive directors or executive members of the governing board of one enterprise, are appointed by the other enterprise; or
(f) more than half of the directors or members of the governing board, or one or more of the executive directors or members of the governing board, of each the two enterprises are appointed by the same person or persons; or
(g) the manufacture or processing of goods or articles or business carried out by one enterprise is wholly dependent on the use of know-how, patents, copyrights, trade-marks, licenses, franchises or any other business or commercial rights of similar nature, or any data, documentation, drawing or specification relating to any patent, invention, model, design, secret formula or process, of which the other enterprise is the

owner or in respect of which the other enterprise has exclusive rights; or

(h) ninety per cent or more of the raw materials and consumables required for the manufacture or processing of goods or articles carried out by one enterprise, are supplied by the other enterprise, or by persons specified by the other enterprise, and the prices and other conditions relating to the supply are influenced by such other enterprise; or

(i) the goods or articles manufactured or processed by one enterprise are sold to the other enterprise or to persons specified by the other enterprise, and the prices and other conditions relating thereto are influenced by such other enterprise; or

(j) where one enterprise is controlled by an individual, the other enterprise is also controlled by such individual or his relative or jointly by such individual and relative of such individual; or

(k) where one enterprise is controlled by a Hindu undivided family, the other enterprise is controlled by a member of such Hindu undivided family, or by a relative of a member of such Hindu undivided family, or jointly by such member and his relative; or

(l) where one enterprise is a firm, associated of persons or body of individuals, the other enterprise holds not less than ten per cent interest in such firm, associated of persons, or body of individuals; or

(m) there exists between the two enterprises, any relationship of mutual interest, as may be prescribed.

Section 92B

Meaning of International Transaction

92(B) (1) For the purposes of this section and sections 92, 92C, 92D an 92E, "international transaction" means a transaction between two or more associated enterprise, either or both of whom are non-residents, in the nature of purchase, sale or lease of tangible or intangible property, or provision of services, or lending or borrowing money, or any other transaction having a bearing on the profits, income, losses or assets of such enterprises, and shall include agreement or arrangement between two or more associated enterprises for the allocation or apportionment of, or any contribution, to any cost or expense incurred or to be incurred in connection with a benefit, service or facility provided or to be provided to any one or more of such enterprises.

(2) A transaction entered into by an enterprise with a person other than an associated enterprise shall, for the purposes of sub-section (1), be deemed to be a transaction entered into between two associated enterprises, if there exists a prior agreement in relation to the relevant transaction between such other person and the associated enterprise, or the terms of the relevant transaction are determined in substance between such other person and the associated enterprise.

Section 92C

Computation of Arm's Length Price

92C. (1) The arm's length price in relation to an international transaction shall be determined by any of the following methods, being the most appropriate method, having regard to the nature of transaction or class of transaction or class of associated persons or functions performed by such persons or such other relevant factors as the Board may prescribe, namely:-

(a) comparable uncontrolled price method;
(b) resale price method;
(c) cost plus method;
(d) profit split method;
(e) transactional net margin method;
(f) such other method as may be prescribed by the Board.

(2) The most appropriate method referred to in sub-section (1) shall be applied, for determination of arm's length price, in the manner as may be prescribed:

Provided that where more than one price may be determined by the most appropriate method, the arm's length price shall be taken to be the arithmetical mean of such prices.

(3) Where during the course of any proceeding for the assessment of income, the Assessing Officer is, on the basis of material or information or document in his possession, of the opinion that-

(a) the price charged or paid in an international transaction has not been determined in accordance with sub-sections(1) and (2); or
(b) any information and document relating to an international transaction have not been kept and maintained by the assessee in accordance with the provisions contained in sub-section(1) of section 92D and the rules made in this behalf; or
(c) the information or data used in computation of the arm's length price is not reliable or correct; or
(d) the assessee has failed to furnish, within the specified time, any information or document which he was required to furnish by a notice issued under sub-section(3) of section 92D.

The Assessing Officer may proceed to determine the arm's length price in relation to the said international transaction in accordance with sub-sections (1) and (2), on the basis of such material or information or document available with him;

Provided that an opportunity shall be given by the Assessing Officer by serving a notice calling upon the assessee to show cause, on a date and time to be specified in the notice, why the arm's length price should not be so determined on the basis of material or information or document in the possession of the Assessing Officer.

(4) Where an arm's length price is determined by the Assessing Officer under sub-section(3), the Assessing Officer may compute the total income of the assessee having regard to the arm's length price so determined:

Provided that no deduction under section 10A or section 10B or under Chapter VIA shall be allowed in respect of the amount of income by which the total income of the assessee is enhanced after computation of income under this sub-section:

Provided further that where the total income of an associated enterprise is computed under this sub-section on determination of the arm's length price paid to another associated enterprise from which tax has been deducted under the provisions of Chapter VXII B, the income of the other associated enterprise shall not be recomputed by reason of such determination of arm's length price in the case of the first mentioned enterprise.

Section 92D

Maintenance and Keeping of Information and Document by Persons Entering into International Transactions

92D (1) Every person who has entered into an international transaction shall keep and maintain such information and document in respect thereof, as may be prescribed.

(2) Without prejudice to the provisions contained in sub-section (1), the Board may prescribe the period for which the information and document shall be kept and maintained under that sub-section.

(3) The Assessing Officer or the Commissioner (Appeals) may, in the course of any proceeding under Act, require any person who has entered into an international transaction to furnish any information or document in respect thereof, as may be prescribed under sub-section (1), within a period of thirty days from the date of receipt of a notice issued in this regard:

Provided that the Assessing Officer or the Commissioner (Appeals) may, on an application made by such person, extend the period of thirty days by a further period not exceeding thirty days.

Section 92E

Report from an Accountant to be Furnished by Persons Entering into International Transaction

92E. Every person who has entered into an international transaction during a previous year shall obtain a report from an accountant and furnish such report on or before the specified date in the prescribed form duly signed and verified in the prescribed manner by such accountant and setting forth such particulars as may be prescribed.

Section 92F

Definitions of Certain Terms Relevant to Computation of Arm's Length Price, etc.

92F. In Sections 92, 92A, 92B, 92C, 92D and 92E, unless the context otherwise requires-

(i) "accountant" shall have the same meaning as in the *Explanation* below sub-section (2) of section 288;

(ii) "arm's length price" means a price which is applied or proposed to be applied in a transaction between persons other than associated enterprises, in uncontrolled conditions;

(iii) "enterprise" means a person(including a permanent establishment of such person) who is, or has been, or is proposed to be, engaged in any activity, relating to the production, storage, supply, distribution, acquisition or control of articles or goods, or know-how, patents, copyrights, trade-marks, licenses, franchises or any other business or commercial rights of similar nature, or any data, documentation, drawing or specification relating to any patent, invention, model, design, secret formula or process, of which the other enterprise is the owner or in respect of which the other enterprise has exclusive rights, or the provision of services of any kind, or in investment, or providing loan or in the business of acquiring, holding, underwriting or dealing with shares, debentures or other securities of any other body corporate whether such activity or business is carried on, directly or through one or more of its units or divisions or subsidiaries, or whether such unit or division or subsidiary is located at the same place where the enterprise is located or at a different place or places;

(iv) "specified date" means

(a) where the assessee is a company, the 31st day of October of the relevant assessment year;

(b) in any other case, the 31st day of July of the relevant assessment year;

(v) "transaction includes an arrangement, understanding or action in concert,-

(a) whether or not such arrangement, understanding or action is formal or in writing, or

(b) whether or not such arrangement, understanding or action is intended to be enforceable by legal proceeding.

Section 271, Explanation 7

Explanation 7 – where in the case of an assessee who has entered into an international transaction defined in section 92B, any amount is added or disallowed in computing the total income under sub-section(4) of section 92C, then, the amount so added or disallowed shall, for the purposes of clause(c) of this sub-section, be deemed to represent the income in respect of which particulars have been concealed or inaccurate particulars have been furnished, unless the assessee proves to the satisfaction of the Assessing Officer or the Commissioner(Appeals) that the price charges or paid in such transaction was computed in accordance with the provisions contained in section 92C and in the manner prescribed under that section, in good faith and with due diligence.

Section 271(1) (C)

Failure to Furnish Returns, Comply with Notices, Concealment of Income etc.

271. (1) If the Assessing Officer or the Commissioner (Appeals) in the course of any proceedings under this Act, is satisfied that any person-

(c) has concealed the particulars of his income or furnished inaccurate particulars of such income.

Section 271 AA

Penalty for Failure to Keep and Maintain Information and Document in Respect of International Transaction

271AA. Without prejudice to the provisions of section 27 1, if any person fails to keep and maintain any such information and document as required by sub-section (1) or sub-section (2) of section 92D, the Assessing Officer or Commissioner (Appeals) may direct that such person shall pay, by way of penalty, a sum equal to two per cent of the value of each international transaction entered into by such person.

Section 271 BA

Penalty for Failure to Furnish Report under Section 92E

271BA. If any person fails to furnish a report from an accountant as required by section 92E, the Assessing Officer may direct that such person shall pay, by way of penalty, a sum of one hundred thousand rupees.

Section 271 G

Penalty for Failure to Furnish Information or Document under Section 92D

271G. If any person who has entered into an international transaction fails to furnish any such information or document as required by sub-section (3) of Section 92D, the Assessing Officer or the Commissioner (Appeals) may direct that such persons hall pay, by way of penalty, a sum equal to two per cent of the value of the international transaction for each such failure.

Section 276 C

Wilful Attempt to Evade Tax, etc.
276C. (1) If a person willfully attempts in any manner whatsoever to evade any tax, penalty or interest chargeable or imposable under this Act, he shall, without prejudice to any penalty that may be imposable on him under any other provision of this Act, be punishable –
(i) in a case where the amount sought to be evaded exceeds one hundred thousand rupees, with rigorous imprisonment for a term which shall not be less than six months but which may extend to seven years and with fine;
(ii) in any other case, with rigorous imprisonment for a term which shall not be less than three months but which may extend to three years and with fine.

(2) If a person willfully attempts in any manner whatsoever to evade the payment of any tax, penalty or interest under this Act, he shall, without prejudice to nay penalty that may be imposable on him under any other provision of this Act, be punishable with rigorous imprisonment for a term which shall not be less than three months but which may extend to three years and shall, in the discretion of the court, also be liable to fine.

Explanation – For the purposes of this section, a willful attempt to evade any tax penalty or interest chargeable or imposable under this Act or the payment thereof shall include a case there any person –
(i) has in his possession or control any books of account or other documents (being books of account or other documents relevant to any proceeding under this Act) containing a false entry or statement; or
(ii) makes or causes to be made any false entry or statement in such books of account or other documents; or
(iii) willfully omits or causes to be omitted any relevant entry or statement in such books of account or other documents; or

(iv) causes any other circumstance to exist which will have the effect of enabling such person to evade any tax, penalty or interest chargeable or imposable under this Act or the payment thereof.

Section 276 D

Failure to Produce Accounts and Documents

276 D. If a person willfully fails to produce, or cause to be produced, on or before the date specified in any notice served on him under sub-section(1) of section 142, such accounts and documents as are referred to in the notice or willfully fails to comply with a direction issued o him under sub-section(2A) of that section, he shall be punishable with rigorous imprisonment for a term which may extend to one year with fine equal to a sum calculated at a rate which shall not be less than four rupees or more than ten rupees for every day during which the default continues, or with both.

Section 277

False Statement in Verification etc.

277. If a person makes a statement in any verification under this Act or under any rule made there under, or delivers an account or statement which is false, and which he either knows or believes to be false, or does not believe to be true, he shall be punishable-

(i) in a case where the amount of tax, which would have been evaded if the statement or account had been accepted as true, exceeds one hundred thousand rupees, with rigorous imprisonment for a term which shall not be less than six months but which may extend to seven years and with fine;

(ii) in any other case, with rigorous imprisonment for a term which shall not be less than three months but which may extend to three years and with fine.

Section 278 B

Offences by Companies

278 B. (1) Where an offence under this Act has been committed by a company, every person who, at the time the offence was committed, was incharge of, and was responsible to, the company for the conduct of the business of the company as well as the company shall be deemed to be guilty of the offence and shall be liable to be proceeded against and punished accordingly:

Provided that nothing contained in this sub-section shall render any such person liable to any punishment if he proves that the offence was committed without his knowledge or that he had exercised all due diligence to prevent the commission of such offence.

(2) Notwithstanding anything contained in sub-section (1), where as offence under this Act has been committed by a company and it is proved that the offence has been committed with the consent or connivance of, or is attributable to any neglect on the part of, any director, manager, secretary or other officer of the company, such director, manager, secretary or other officer shall also be deemed to be guilty of that offence and shall be liable to be proceeded against and punished accordingly.

Explanation – For the purposes of this section, -

(a) "company" means a body corporate, and includes -
   (i) a firm; and
   (ii) an association of persons or a body of individuals whether incorporated or not; and

(b) "director", in relation to-
   (i) a firm, means a partner in the firm;
   (ii) any association of persons or a body of individuals, means any member controlling the affairs thereof.

Appendix 2

New Transfer Pricing Rules

In exercise of powers conferred by section 295, read with sections 92C, 92D and 92E of the Income-tax Act, 1961 (43 of 1961), the Central Government hereby makes the following rules further to amend the Income-tax rules, 1962, namely-

1. (i) These rules may be called the Income-tax (21st Amendment) Rules, 2001

(ii) They shall come into force on the date of their publication in the official Gazette.

2. In the Income-tax Rules, 1962, -

(i) after rule 10, the following rules shall be inserted, namely:-

"10A. *Meaning of expressions used in computation of arm's length price* – For the purposes of this rule and rules 10B to 10E, -

(a) 'uncontrolled transaction' means a transaction between enterprises other than associated enterprises, whether resident or non-resident;

(b) 'property' includes goods, articles or things, or intangible property;

(c) 'services' include financial services;

(d) 'transaction' includes a number of closely linked transactions.

10B. *Determination of arm's length price under section 92C* - (1) For the purposes of sub-section(2) of section 92C, the arm's length price in relation to an international transaction shall be determined by any of the following methods, being the most appropriate method, in the following manner, namely:-

(a) comparable uncontrolled price method, by which, -

(i) the price charged or paid for property transferred or services provided in a comparable uncontrolled transaction, or a number of such transactions, is identified;

(ii) such price is adjusted to account for differences, if any, between the international transaction and the comparable uncontrolled transactions or between the enterprises entering into such transaction, which could materially affect the price in the open market;

(iii) the adjusted price arrived at under sub-clause(ii) is taken to be an arm's length price in respect of the properly transferred or services provided in the international transaction;

(b) resale price method, by which;-

(i) the price at which property purchased or services obtained by the enterprise from an associated enterprise is resold or are provided to an unrelated enterprise, is identified;

(ii) such resale price is reduced by the amount of a normal gross profit margin accruing to the enterprise or to an unrelated enterprise from the purchase and resale of the same or similar property or from obtaining and providing the same or similar services, in a comparable uncontrolled transaction, or a number of such transactions;

(iii) the price so arrived at is further reduced by the expenses incurred by the enterprise in connection with the purchase of property or obtaining of services;

(iv) the price so arrived at is adjusted to take into account the functional and other differences, including differences in accounting practices, if any, between the international transaction and the comparable uncontrolled transactions, or between the enterprises entering into such transactions, which could materially affect the amount of gross profit margin in the open market;

(v) the adjusted price arrived at under sub-clause(iv) is taken to be an arm's length price in respect of the purchase of the property or obtaining of the services by the enterprise from the associated enterprise;

(c) cost plus method, by which,-

(i) the direct and indirect costs of production incurred by the enterprise in respect of property transferred or services provided to an associated enterprise, are determined;

(ii) the amount of a normal gross profit mark-up to such costs (computed according to the same accounting norms) arising from the transfer or provision of the same or similar property or services by the enterprise, or by an unrelated enterprise, in a comparable uncontrolled transaction, or a number of such transactions, is determined;

(iii) the normal gross profit mark-up referred to in sub-clause (ii) is adjusted to take into account the functional and other differences, if any, between the international transaction and the comparable uncontrolled transactions, or between the enterprises entering into such transactions, which could materially affect such profit mark-up in the open market;

(iv) the costs referred to in sub-clause(i) are increased by the adjusted profit mark-up arrived at under sub-clause (iii);

(v) the sum so arrived at is taken to be an arm's length price in relation to the supply of the property or provision of services by the enterprise;

(d) profit split method, which may be applicable mainly in international transactions involving transfer of unique intangibles or in multiple international transactions which are so inter related that they cannot be evaluated separately for the purpose of determining the arm's length price of any one transaction, by which -

(i) the combined net profit of the associated enterprises arising from the international transaction in which they are engaged, is determined;

(ii) the relative contribution made by each of the associated enterprises to the earning of such combined net profit, is then evaluated on the basis of the functions performed, assets employed or to be employed and risks assumed by each enterprise and on the basis of reliable external market data which indicates how such contribution would be evaluated by unrelated enterprises performing comparable functions in similar circumstances;

(iii) the combined net profit is then split amongst the enterprises in proportion to their relative contributions, as evaluated under sub-clause(ii);

(iv) the profit thus apportioned to the assessee is taken into account to arrive at an arm's length price in relation to the international transaction:

Provided that the combined net profit referred to in sub-clause(i) may, in the first instance, be partially allocated to each enterprise so as to provide it with a basic return appropriate for the type of international transaction in which it is engaged, with reference to market returns achieved for similar types of transactions by independent enterprises, and thereafter, the residual net profit remaining after such allocation may be split amongst the enterprises in proportion to their relative contribution in the manner specified under sub-clauses(ii) and (iii), and in such a case the aggregate of the net profit allocated to the enterprise in the first instance together with the residual net profit apportioned to that enterprise on the basis of its relative contribution shall be taken to be the net profit arising to that enterprise from the international transaction;

(e) transactional net margin method, by which, -

(i) the net profit margin realised by the enterprise from an international transaction entered into with an associated enterprise is computed in relation to costs incurred or sales effected or assets employed or to be employed by the enterprise or having regard to any other relevant base;

(ii) the net profit margin realised by the enterprise or by an unrelated enterprise from a comparable uncontrolled transaction or a number of such transactions is computed having regard to the same base;

(iii) the net profit margin referred to in sub-clause(ii) arising in comparable uncontrolled transactions is adjusted to take into account the differences, if any, between the international transaction and the comparable uncontrolled transaction, or between the enterprises entering into such transactions, which could materially affect the amount of net profit margin in the open market;

(iv) the net profit margin realised by the enterprise and referred to in sub-clause(i) is established to be the same as the net profit margin referred to in sub-clause(iii);

(v) the net profit margin thus established is then taken into account to arrive at an arm's length price in relation to the international transaction.

(2) For the purposes of sub-rule (1), the comparability of an international transaction with an uncontrolled transaction shall be judged with reference to the following, namely:-

(a) the specific characteristics of the property transferred or service provided in either transaction,

(b) the functions performed, taking into account assets employed or to be employed and the risks assumed, by the respective parties to the transactions;

(c) the contractual terms (whether or not such terms are formal or in writing) of the transactions which lay down explicitly or implicitly how the responsibilities, risks and benefits are to be divided between the respective parties to the transactions;

(d) conditions prevailing in the markets in which the respective parties to the transactions operate, including the geographical location and size of the markets, the laws and Government orders in force, costs of labour and capital in the markets, overall economic development and level of competition and whether the markets are wholesale or retail.

(3) An uncontrolled transaction shall be comparable to an international transaction, if,-

(i) none of the differences, if any, between the transactions being compared, or between the enterprises entering into such transactions are likely to materially affect the price or cost charged or paid in, or the profit arising from, such transactions in the open market; or

(ii) reasonably accurate adjustments can be made to eliminate the material effects of such differences.

(4) The data to be used in analysing the comparability of an uncontrolled transaction with an international transaction shall be the data relating to the financial year in which the international transaction has been entered into:

Provided that data relating to a period not being more than two years prior to such financial year may also be considered if such data reveals facts which could have an influence on the determination of transfer prices in relation to the transactions being compared.

10C. *Most appropriate method* – (1) For the purposes of sub-section(1) of section 92C, the most appropriate method shall be the method which is best suited to the facts and circumstances of each particular international transaction, and which provides the most reliable measure of an arm's length price in relation to the international transaction.

(2) In selecting the most appropriate method as specified in sub-rule (1), the following factors shall be taken into account, namely:-

(a) the nature and class of the international transaction;

(b) the class or classes of associated enterprises entering into the transaction and the functions performed by them taking into account assets employed or to be employed and risks assumed by such enterprises;

(c) the availability, coverage and reliability of data necessary for application of the method;

(d) the degree of comparability existing between the international transaction and the uncontrolled transaction and between the enterprises entering into such transactions;

(e) the extent to which reliable and accurate adjustments can be made to account for differences, if any, between the international transaction and the comparable uncontrolled transaction or between the enterprises entering into such transactions;

(f) the nature, extent and reliability of assumptions required to be made in application of a method.

10D. *Information and documents to be kept and maintained under section 92D* – (1) Every person who has entered into an international transaction shall keep and maintain the following information and documents, namely;-

a) a description of the ownership structure of the assessee enterprise with details of shares or other ownership interest held therein by other enterprises;
b) a profile of the multinational group of which the assessee enterprise is a part along with the name, address, legal status and country of tax residence of each of the enterprises comprised in the group with whom international transactions have been entered into by the assessee, and ownership linkages among them;
c) a broad description of the business of the assessee and the industry in which the assessee operates, and of the business of the associated enterprises with whom the assessee has transacted.
d) the nature and terms (including prices) of international transactions entered into with each associated enterprise, details of property transferred or services provided and the quantum and the value of each such transaction or class of such transaction;
e) a record of the economic and market analyses, forecasts, budgets or any other financial estimates prepared by the assessee for the business as a whole and for each division or product separately, which may have a bearing on the international transactions entered into by the assessee;
f) a record of uncontrolled transactions taken into account for analysing their comparability with the international transactions entered into, including a record of the nature, terms and conditions relating to any uncontrolled transaction with third parties which may be of relevance to the pricing of the international transactions;
g) a record of the analysis performed to evaluate comparability of uncontrolled transactions with the relevant international transaction;
h) a description of the methods considered for determining the arm's length price in relation to each international transaction or class of transaction, the method selected as the most appropriate method along with explanations as to why such

method was so selected, and how such method was applied in each case;

i) a record of the actual working carried out for determining the arm's length price, including details of the comparable data and financial information used in applying the most appropriate method, and adjustments, if any, which were made to account for differences between the international transaction and the comparable uncontrolled transactions, or between the enterprises entering into such transactions;

j) the assumptions, policies and price negotiations, if any, which have critically affected the determination of the arm's length price;

k) details of the adjustments, if any, made to transfer prices to align them with arm's length prices determined under these rules and consequent adjustment made to the total income for tax purposes;

l) any other information, data or document, including information or data relating to the associated enterprise, which may be relevant for determination of the arm's length price.

(2) Nothing contained in sub-rule(1) shall apply in a case where the aggregate value, as recorded in the books of account, of international transactions entered into by the assessee does not exceed one crore rupees;

Provided that the assessee shall be required to substantiate, on the basis of material available with him, that income arising from international transactions entered into by him has been computed in accordance with Section 92.

(3) The information specified in sub-rule (1) shall be supported by authentic documents, which may include the following:

(a) official publications, reports, studies and data bases from the Government of the country of residence of the associated enterprise, or of any other country;

(b) reports of market research studies carried out and technical publications brought out by institutions of national or international repute;
(c) priced publications including stock exchange and commodity market quotations;
(d) published accounts and financial statements relating to the business affairs of the associated enterprise;
(e) agreements and contracts entered into with associated enterprises or with unrelated enterprises in respect of transactions similar to the international transactions;
(f) letters and other correspondence documenting any terms negotiated between the assessee and the associated enterprise;
(g) documents normally issued in connection with various transactions under the accounting practices followed.

(4) The information and documents specified under sub-rules (1) and (2), should, as far as possible, be contemporaneous and should exist latest by the specified date referred to in clause (iv) of section 92F.

Provided that where an international transaction continues to have effect over more than one previous years, fresh documentation need not be maintained separately in respect of each previous year, unless there is any significant change in the nature or terms of the international transaction, in the assumptions made, or in any other factor which could influence the transfer price, and in case of such significant change, fresh documentation as may be necessary under sub-rules (1) and (2) shall be maintained bringing out the impact of the change on the pricing of the international transaction.

(5) The information and documents specified in sub-rules (1) and (2) shall be kept and maintained for a period of eight years from the end of the relevant assessment year.

10E. *Report from an accountant to be furnished under Section 92E* - The report from an accountant required to be furnished under section 92E be every person who has entered into an international transaction during a previous year shall be in Form No.3CEB and be verified in the manner indicated therein".

(ii) Rule 11 shall be omitted.

(iii) in the Appendix, after Form No.3CEA, the following Form shall be inserted, namely:-

Form No. 3CEB
(See Rule 10 E)

Report from an accountant to be furnished under section 92E Relating to international transaction(s)

1. *I/We have examined the accounts and records of .... (name and address of the assessee with PAN) relating to the international transactions entered into by the assessee during the previous year ending on 31st March, ...

2. In *my/our opinion proper information and documents as are prescribed have been kept by the assessee in respect of the international transaction(s) entered into so far as appears from *my/our examination of the records of the assessee.

3. The particulars required to be furnished under section 92E are given in the Annexure to this Form. In *my/our opinion and to the best of my/our information and according to the explanations given to *me/us, the particulars given in the Annexure are true and correct.

....
** Signed ....
Name ....
Address: ....
....
Membership No.:...........

Place: ....
Date: ....

Notes

1. *Delete whichever is not applicable
2. **This report has to be signed by –

(i) a chartered accountant within the meaning of Chartered Accountants Act, 1949 (38 of 1949); or
(ii) any person who in relation to any state, is, by virtue of the provisions in sub-section(2) of section 226 of the companies Act, 1956 (1 of 1956), entitled to be appointed to act an as auditor of companies registered in that State.

Annexure to Form No. 3CEB

Particulars Relating to International Transactions required to be Furnished under Section 92E of the Income-Tax Act, 1961

PART A

1. Name of the assessee
2. Address
3. Permanent Account Number
4. Status
5. Previous year ended
6. Assessment year

PART B

7. List of associated enterprises with whom the assessee has entered into international transactions, with the following details:
   - (a) Name of the associated enterprise
   - (b) Nature of the relationship with the associated enterprise as referred to in section 92A (2)
   - (c) Brief description of the business carried on by the associated enterprise.

8. Particulars in respect of transactions in tangible property

A. Has the assessee entered into any international Transaction(s) in respect of purchase / sale of Raw material, consumables or any other supplies For assembling/processing/manufacturing of Goods/articles from/to associated enterprises? *Yes / No*

If yes, provide the following details in respect of Each associated enterprise and each transaction Or class of transaction:

(a) Name and address of the associated Enterprise with whom the international Transaction has been entered into

(b) Description of transaction and quantity Purchased /sold.

(c) Total amount paid/received or payable/ Receivable in the transaction –

(i) as per books of account.

(ii) as computed by the assessee having regard to the arm's length price.

(d) Method used for determining the arm's length price

B. Has the assessee entered into any international transaction(s) In respect of purchase/sale of traded /finished goods? *Yes / No*

If yes, provide the following details in respect of each Associated enterprise and each transaction or class of Transaction:

(a) Name and address of the associated enterprise With whom the international transaction has been Entered into

(b) Description of transaction and quantity Purchased /sold.

(c) Total amount paid/received or payable /

Receivable in the transaction –
(i) as per books of account
(ii)as computed by the assessee having regard
to the arm's length price.
(d) Method used for determining the arm's length
Price [see section 92C (1)]

C. Has the assessee entered into any international transaction(s) In respect of purchase/sale of any other tangible movable/ Immovable property or lease of such property? *Yes / No*

If yes provide the following details in respect of each Associated enterprise and each transaction or class of transaction

(a) Name and address of the associated enterprise with whom The international transaction has been entered into
(b) Description of the property of movable/immovable Property involved in the transaction
(c) Number of units of each category of movable/immovable Property involved in the transaction
(d) amount paid/received or payable/receivable in each transaction of purchase/sale, or lease rent paid/received or payable/receivable in respect of each lease provided/entered into –
(i) as per books of account
(ii) as computed by the assessee having regard to the arm's length price.
(e) Method used for determining the arm's length Price [See section 92C (1)]

9. Particulars in respect of transactions in intangible property:
Has the assessee entered into any international Transaction(s) in respect of purchase/sale/use of Intangible property such as know-how, patents, Copyrights, licenses, etc.? *Yes / No*

If yes, provide the following details in respect of Each associated enterprise and each category of Intangible property:

(a) Name and address of the associated enterprise With whom the international transaction has Been entered into

(b) Description of intangible property and nature Of transaction

(c) Amount paid/received or payable/receivable For purchase/sale/use of each category of Intangible property –

(i) as per books of accounts

(ii) as computed by the assessee having regard to the arm's length price.

(d) Method used for determining the arm's length Price [see section 92C (1)]

10. Particulars in respect of providing of services: Has the assessee entered into any international Transaction(s) in respect of services such as Financial, administrative, technical, commercial Services, etc.? *Yes / No*

If yes, provide the following details in respect of Each associated enterprise and each category of Service:

(a) name and address of the associated enterprise with whom the international transaction has been entered into

(b) Description of services provided/availed to/from the associated enterprise

(c) Amount paid/received or payable/receivable for the services provided/taken –

   (i) as per books of account

   (ii) as computed by the assessee having regard to the arm's length price.

(e) method used for determining the arm's length price
[see section 92C (1)]

11. Particulars in respect of lending or borrowing money:
Has the assessee entered into any international transaction
In respect of granting/receiving loans/advances to or from
Associated enterprise? *Yes / No*

If yes, provide the following details in respect of each
Associated enterprise and each loan/advances;

(a) Name and address of the associated enterprise
With whom the international transaction has been
entered into.
(b) Nature of financing agreement
(c) Currency in which loan/advance granted/received
(d) Interest rate charged/paid in respect of each loan/
Advance.
(e) Amount paid/received or payable/receivable in the
Transaction –
(i) as per books of account
(ii) as computed by the assessee having regard to
the arm's length price.
(f) Method used for determining the arm's length price
[see section92C (1)].

12. Particulars in respect of mutual agreement or arrangement
Has the assessee entered into any international transaction
With an associated enterprise or enterprises by way of
A mutual agreement or arrangement for the allocation or
Apportionment of, or any contribution to, any cost or
Expense incurred or to be incurred in connection with a
Benefit, service or facility provided or to be provided to
Any one or more of such enterprises? *Yes / No*

If yes, provide the following details in respect of each
Agreement/arrangement:

(a) name and address of the associated enterprise with whom the international transaction has been entered into.
(b) Description of such mutual agreement or arrangement
(c) amount paid/received or payable/receivable in each such transaction –
  (i) as per books of account
  (ii) as computed by the assessee having regard to the arm's length price.
(d) Method used for determining the arm's length Price [See section 92C (1)]

13. Particulars in respect of any other transaction; Has the assessee entered into ay other international Transaction not specifically referred to above, with Associated enterprise? *Yes / No*

If yes, provide the following details in respect of each Associate enterprise and each transaction:
(a) Name and address of the associated enterprise with whom the international transaction has been entered into.
(b) Description of the transaction.
(c) Amount paid/received or payable/receivable in the transaction –
  (i) as per books of account.
  (ii) as computed by the assessee having regard to the arm's length price.
(e) method used for determining the arm's length price [see section 92C (1)]

....
*Signed.................
Name:..................
Address:................
....

Place: ....
Date: ....

Notes: **This annexure has to be signed by –
(i) a chartered accountant within the meaning of Chartered Accountants Act, 1949 (38 of 1949); or
(ii) any person who in relation to any state, is, by virtue of the provisions in sub-section (2) of section 226 of the companies Act, 1956 (1 of 1956), entitled to be appointed to act an as auditor of companies registered in that State.

Notification No.: S.O.808 (E), *dated 21.8.2001.*

Bibliography

Bibliography

BOOKS

1. Anton, Hector, R., and other (Ed.), *Contemporary Issues in Cost and Managerial Accounting* (Boston, Houghton Mifflin Company, 1978), Chapter 24-25.
2. Arpon, J.S., *International Incorporate Pricing Non-American System and Views* (New York, Praeger, 1972)
3. Belkaoul, Ahmed, *Cost Accounting: A Multi Dimensional Emphasis,* Chapter 13.
4. Black, Homer A., and Edwards, James Don, *The Managerial and Cost Accountants Hand Book* – Chapter 13.
5. Blerman, Harold, Jr., and Dyckman, Thomson R., *Managerial Cost Accounting* (New York, Macmillan Publishing Co. Inc., 1976) Chapter 19.
6. Choi, Frederic, D.S., and Muller Gerhard, G., *International Accounting* – (Englewood Cliffs, New Jersey, Prentice-Hall Inc., 1992), Chapter II.
7. Daniels, John, D., Ernest, W. Organ, Jr., and Lee, H., Rade Baugh, *International Business: Environment and Operations,* 2nd ed. Reading, (Wesley, Mass: Addison- 1979).
8. Dearden, John, *Cost Accounting and Financial System* (California, Addison, Wesley Publishing Company, 1973) Chapter 10.
9. Fisher, Paul, M., and Frank, Werner, G., *Cost Accounting: Theory and Application.*
10. Ganguli, B.N., *Multinational Corporation,* Chapter 14 – pp. 1-10 and pp. 28-46.
11. Hartley, Ronald V., *Cost and Managerial Accounting* Chapter 20.
12. Hansen, Don R., and Mowen, Aryanne, M., *Management Accounting,* Chapter 17, 7th Edition.
13. Heitger, L.E., and Motalich, S., *Management Accounting* (Japan, McGraw Hill International, 1982).

14. Horngreen, Charles, T., *Cost Accounting – A Managerial Emphasis* (New Delhi, Prentice Hall of India, 1991), Chapter 22.
15. Horngreen, Charles, T., *Introduction to Management Accounting,* (U.S.A. Prentice Hall International Edition, 1981) Chapter 10.
16. *Income Tax Act* (New Delhi, Taxman Allied Services, 2000).
17. Kaplan, R., and Atkinson, A.A., *Advanced Management Accounting,* 2nd Edition, (Englewood Cliffs, New Jersey, Prentice Hall Inc., 1989).
18. Lall, Rajiv, B., *Multinational from the Third World* (Oxford, Oxford University Press, 1986).
19. Lall Sanjay, *Multinational Corporation: Nine Essays* (London, Macmillian, 1980)
20. Lall Sanjay, and Slreetan Paul, *Foreign Investment, Transnational and Developing Countries'* (London, Macmillan, 1977).
21. Maher, Deakin, *Cost Accounting, pp.* 861 – 891.
22. Matz, Adolph, Curry, J., Othel, and Frank, George, W., *Cost Accounting* (Cincinnati, South Western Publishing Co., 1976) Chapter 29.
23. Mittal, D.P., *Law of Transfer Pricing* (New Delhi, Taxman Allied Services, 2001), Chapter 2, 3 and 4.
24. Morse, Wayne, J., *Cost Accounting,* Second Edition, Chapter 19.
25. Organisation for Economic Cooperation and Development, *Transfer Pricing and Multinational Enterprises* (Paris, OECD, 1979).
26. Rathore, Shirin, *International Accounting* (New Delhi, Prentice Hall of India, 1996), Chapter 10.
27. Rugman, A.M., *Inside the Multinationals* (New York, Columbia University Press, 1981), Page 84.
28. Sen, S.C., *Multinational Corporations in the Developing Countries* (Calcutta: Eastern Law House, 1978).
29. Sharan, V., *International Financial Management* (New Delhi, Prentice – Hall of India, 2001) Chapter 23, Pages 386-396.

30. Shilling Law, G., and Burton, J.C., *Management and Profit Centre Concept, Management Accounting Bulletin 4*, (American Management Association, 1964).
31. Siddharthan, N.S., *Conglomerates and Multinationals in India.*
32. Solomons, David, *Divisional Performance: Measurement and Control* (Homewood, III: Irwin 1965).
33. Shilling Law, *Cost Accounting Analysis and Control* Chapter 26.
34. Tang, Roger, Y.W.C.K. Walter, and Robert, H., Raymond, *Transfer Pricing – Japanese vs. American Style, Management Accounting* (January 1979) pages 12-16.
35. Varshney, R.L., and Bhashyam, S., *International Financial Management- An Indian Perspective* (New Delhi, Sultan Chand & Sons, 2001) Chapter 14, page 354 to 355.
36. Verlage, H.C., *Transfer Pricing for Multinational Enterprises,* Netherlands, Rotterdam University Press, 1975.

JOURNALS AND ARTICLES

1. Abdel-Khalek, A. Rashad and Edward J.Lusk, *Transfer Pricing – A Synthesis,* Accounting Review 49, No.1 (Jan 1974) 8-23.
2. Bhattacharya, Prasenjit, *India's Transfer Pricing Norms Faulty,* the Economic Times, March 9, 2001.
3. Ballarpur Industries Limited, *Annual Report*, 1992-93, Delhi.
4. Baumol, W.J., and Fabian, T., *Decomposition, Pricing for Decentralised and External Economies.* Management Science, Vol.10, pp. 1-31, July 1964.
5. Cowen, S.S., Phillips, L.C., and Stillabower, L., *Multinational Transfer Pricing,* Management Accounting, Vol. 60 No.7, pp. 17-22, January 1979.

6. Confederation of Indian Industry, *Getting Transfer Pricing Right,* Confederation of Indian Industry, New Delhi, July 2001.
7. Dabur India Ltd., *Annual Report*, 1999-2000, Delhi.
8. Dasgupta, S., *Juggling Numbers,* India Today, p.133, September 30, 1993.
9. Godfrey James, T., *Short-Run Planning in a Decentralised Firm,* Accounting Review 46, No.2 (April 1971), pp. 286-297.
10. Goetz, Billy, E., *Transfer Pricing: An Exercise in Relevancy and Goal Congruence,* Accounting Review 42, No.3 (July 1967), pp. 430-440.
11. Govindarajan, V., and Ramamurthy, B., *Transfer Pricing Policies in Indian Companies*, The Chartered Accountant PP 296-301, Nov. 1983.
12. Hirshleifer, Jack, *On the Economics of Transfer Pricing,* Journal of Business 29, No.3 (July 1956), pages 172-184.
13. Iyengar, Jayanthi, *Transfer Pricing MNC Tax Woe No1,* the Economic Times, Nov. 18, 1999.
14 JK Industries Ltd., *Annual Report*, 1999-2000, Delhi.
15. Kably, Luria, *Transfer Pricing Norms Update on Cards,* The Economic Times Nov. 9, 1999.
16. Kapardia, S., and Marwaha, K., *West Foot Forward: Transfer Pricing Norms in the US and UK*, The Economic Times, Feb. 5, 2001, p. 13.
17 Kapardia Sudhir, and Marwaha Kapil, *Transfer Pricing: Playing for Global Sweep Stakes* The Economic Times, Feb. 5, 2001, p. 12.
18 Keagan D.P., and Howard, P.D., *Making Transfer Prices Work for Services,* The Journal of Accountancy, Vol. 165, No.3, pp 96-103, March 1988.
19 Kim, S.H., and Miller, S.W., *Constituents of International Transfer Pricing Divisions,* Columbia, Journal of World Business, pp. 71-72, Spring 1979.

20. Manes, Rene P., *Birch Paper Company Revisited: An Exercise in Transfer Pricing,* Accounting Review 45, No. 3, (July 1970), pp. 565-591.

21. Merville, Larry J., and William Pelty, *Transfer Pricing for the Multinational firms,* Accounting Review 53, No. 4(Oct. 1978), pp. 935-951.

22. National Association of Accountants, NAA, Research Report 30, *Accounting for Intra Company Transfer,* New York: National Association of Accountants.

23. Padmakshan, M., *CBEC Trans Gun on Transfer Pricing,* The Economic Times, June 15, 2000.

24. Ranbaxy Laboratories Ltd., *Annual Report*, 1999-2000, Delhi.

25. Shah, Rajiv, *Principles of Transfer Pricing,* The Chartered Accountants, Jan. 2000.

26. Sharav, I., *Transfer Pricing – Diversity of goods and practices, The Journal of Accountancy*, Vol. 138, pp 56-62, April 1974.

27. Taylor, R., and Hendricks, R., *U.S. Advance Pricing Agreements,* Accountancy, Vol. 32, p.56, October 1991.

28. Tax Bureau, Ministry of Finance, *An outline of Japanese Tax*, p.100, 1986.

29. *US Treasury Regulation,* Sec. 482-1.

WEBSITES VISITED

1. http://www taxnewscom/t
2. http:// royalty stat.com/articles2.cfm
3. http://www.oecd.org/daf/fa/tr price/transfer.htm
4. http://www.xbsolutions .com/pricepoint scenarios.html
5. http://www.pathfinder.com/asiaweek/96/0119/bizl.html
6. http://www.us.kpmg.com/ecs/tpspec.html
7. http://wwwfinacialexpress.com/fe/daily/19990303/feo 03022 html
8. http://www.uskpmg.com/ecs/tp.html

9. http://www/infoindia.com/bo/iw/ip 00606 html
10 http://www/baclass.panam.edu/courses/iulb 4365/definitions-
11 http://wehner.tamn.edu.mgmt.www/mgmt.667/667-QUE-WK11.html
12. http://www.unrisdog/engindex/publ/list/op/op5/op05-03 htm
13 http:www.economics.tcd.ie/ser/1998/Essay15.htm
14 http://casenet.thomson com/casenet/abstracts/selected-mtp html
15 http://www/maruliduyog.com/about2.htm
16 http://www.laucs.ac.uk/users/law/intlaw/ibuslaw/docs/lr-tp.htm

Index

Index